Behind the Muffler

Robert J. Frey
plus
A Summary of Obsolete Words
by
Norbert McGuire

Behind the Muffler
Third Edition

Published through Lulu Press, Inc.

All rights reserved
Copyright ©2017 by Robert I. Frey

ISBN: 978-1-387-02280-9

To Caleb and Abe Frey, 2017

The early homo sapiens probably needed only six or eight words to maintain their lives. Ought oh, hunt oh, uh huh, wheee, whoops, wow, aye, yeye yeye, yeye, yiii and humph.

Using less than a dozen letters and little effort these words (if you can call them words) were easy to say but are difficult to spell. But alas, these few terms could not convey humor, gossip, teasing, jokes and curses so language was further developed and then later on writing. Paper was created to record these essentials of humanity, although engraved rocks have lasted better.

So join with me in these reminisces and bear with me, a semi-retired dairy farmer, who grew up during the tail end of the Great Depression and who has an interest in antique tractors, old cars and people and their eccentricities. For the reader, I may not be politically correct but I've tried not to be vulgar. Enjoy, and perhaps you may be inspired to write down some of your own stories. After all, your tombstone will only preserve your dates of birth and death, and your stories will die with you. So, I dedicate these tales to my teenage grandsons, who at some time in the distant future may develop an interest in local history. They did contribute to the twenty-first technology used for these pages, and I wish you guys the best.

Acknowledgements

To Albina Morris, who got me started writing for the Antique Automobile Club of America's Lehigh Valley Newsletter.

To Denise Conroy and Mary Jane Pokojni who deciphered my scribbles.

To my late grade school buddy, Norbert McGuire for some ideas, obsolete words and lost arts.

To Sandy Hager for sharing her artwork.

I am grateful to Trish Becker, Sue Tintle and Ingrid Gray for editing.

Thank you, Dr. Bob Briglia, for the Lindburg story.

It is nice to have good friends, and I certainly do appreciate your good friendship.

Also thanks to Milly Rice for typing all this stuff onto a Twenty-First Century 'stick' since I am at best a Nineteenth Century Renaissance man.

Of course, I can't forget my wife, Trudy (The Quilt Lady) who tolerates papers strewn all over our house. Plus, my sons, Bruce and Rob and grandsons Caleb and Abe who all helped in their own ways.

Bob Frey

Bob Frey, Chippy and '31 Chevy, circa 1939.

Foreword
By Bruce Frey

Once in a while, I figure out a good gift. It's particularly hard finding a gift for my parents who don't really want anything, don't need anything, and have enough junk left over from previous generations that there is little room for more.

But I did well on their 50th Anniversary Party in 2011. I compiled a group of what I felt were the best stories written by my father (originally printed in our local Antique Car Club newsletter) and had them published in a book called *Behind the Motometer*. The little blue paperback was given to all the guests. Since then, my father has proudly handed copies to friends and even sold some at antique car meets. If you don't have one, let him know, or... you can find one on Amazon.com.

Soon he was talking about a second publication, the tome currently in your hands. His plan was to have *Behind the Muffler* ready for his Model T's 100th Birthday Party on June 25th, 2017. He spent many hours working on it: whenever he wasn't repairing something, driving something, reading something or taking a nap. This is his project. It is his baby. His magnus opus. I have had little to do with it until this past week, but the week has been a fun one. We had a good laugh as we tried to put into print the old unwritten family recipe of oyster pie. (1) Best of luck when baking that. Dad and I never have.

Much like a fat slice of Grandma's homemade oyster pie, this book is a gift, enjoyed in the present, yet harkening back across the generations. It is a gift from Robert I. Frey of stories that would soon be forgotten had he not written them down.

Enjoy with some warm milk and dab of butter.

Bob and Trudy at their 50th wedding anniversary deciding who is going to lead.

(1) See "Oysters" on page 72

YOU DON'T HAVE TO BE A FARMER, BUT IT HELPS

When you are behind the muffler
You can discover
All kinds of interesting things,
Like smells of springs,
And of skunks and nitrous oxide,
Of blow-by and carbon monoxide,
That rock I hit most every year
Must be right around here.
"Ka-bang"
Damn – another broken plow share!
That cumulus cloud off to the west
Probably won't leave at my behest
And I'll get a wet arse,
Although rainfall has been sparse.
A cab tractor would be nice
But I cannot afford the price
With Grandpap eighty years ago
At a big Farmall we looked in awe
And knew we would not afford it at all.
Now I don't have the quarter mil' to spend
But I owe no more now than I did then.

LOST ARTS

of making a proper cup of tea
of pulling rhubarb
of saying grace
of whittling
of making souse
of chivalry
of harnessing a team
of contrition
of gigging for eels
of eating chitlins
of investigative reporting
of practical jokes
of credibility
of greasing one's own car
of political incorrectness
of tying miller's knots
of double clutching
of making switzel
of making homemade root beer
of making homemade bread
of unrolling barb wire
of husking corn
of hoeing weeds
of hunting eggs
of butchering
of making oyster pie

of using a hand clutch

of wielding an Austrian scythe

of making a cat's cradle

of using a thunder mug

of using a privy

of reading a daily paper

of cleaning the chicken coop

of cooking on a kerosene stove

of making corn fritters

of pushing a reel mower

of taking out the ashes

of cranking an ice cream churn

of cranking a 2-cylinder John Deere

of cranking a car

of priming a pitcher pump

of taking down storm windows

of using a hat pin

of planting, according to phase of moon

of making corn liquor

of slopping the hogs

of clipping the cows

of hanging clothes to dry

of beating rugs

of wearing white gloves and hats to church

of using Porter's Salve

of whistling

of using a whetstone

of churning butter

of shifting gears in a Model "T" Ford
of playing the family organ
of digging post holes
of using lard to make pie crust
of sleeping in church
of twiddling your thumbs
of thumbing your nose
of using a Kodak Brownie
of sweeping the sidewalk

(For More Lost Arts, see page 184)

Model T running "thrashing" machine.

'Geezer Tour'

There I was, sitting on a park bench in Alaska waiting for both my wife and the Yukon and White Pass narrow gauge railroad that takes modern day tourists up the mountain that the gold miners climbed in the nineteenth century. I was watching a rush of twenty-first century folks hurrying from our cruise ship to buy their gold trinkets (fool's gold?) from the many gift shops in downtown Skagway. And then I saw a shiny yellow bus hauling tourists that was being driven by a lady in a long skirt. It looked a lot like the 1932 Chevy school bus I rode to high school, but it had a grill somewhat like a 1937 Packard.

The following week, I saw a similar bus on that same 'Geezer' Tour, at Yellowstone National Park. Being me, I crawled under it and figured out it was a first-class Retro/Restoration. Somewhere I had heard that Ford Motor Company had, in the late 1990's (when Fomoco Stock was well above the current 8), retrofitted old Park Service buses with modern chassis, transmissions and propane burning engines.

Fast forward to August 2007 and another tour with a stop at the elegant Prince of Wales Hotel, where I saw several similar red buses and had time to get a good close look. They had 1936 White Truck styling and were restored buses that the National Park Service had been using for years. They were equipped with eight doors, folding tops a la Citroen 2 CV and leather seats that could seat five across. In this particular case, they were being used to shuttle tourists back and forth from the Canadian portion of Glacier National Park to the American portion of Rocky Mountain National Park.

I eventually found out that in the early 1930's the United Sates Government had, in military fashion, requested bids for 98 busses to transport tourists throughout the National Park system. Various manufacturers submitted bids. Test vehicles were required to haul sand bags up through the Rocky Mountains. White Motor Trucks won with their long stroke, 318 cubic-inch, engines but the contracts called for 'modern' design and White Trucks had hardly changed styling since World War I. Industrial designer Count Alexis De Sakhnoffsky was contacted. They created styling that was typical of 1930's Art Deco, with a cascading Packard type grill, enclosed rear fenders, bulbous front fenders with tear drop headlights and rear end treatment like Dave Schomp's 1937 black Ford. Sakhnoffsky had worked on the design of American Bantam, Cord, Auburn Nash and Packard and created a nice timeless design for White. I don't know if the old Park Service busses are technically Retro/Restored or Refurbished.

Behind the Poetic Muffler

If your wife is shopping hell bent- Oh
And to her some money you lent –Oh
Your Visa card she did confiscate – Oh
Sit and watch the pretty girls and placate- OOOh

Ubiquitous Plastic

Everything we buy is sealed hermetically,
Like car parts, scissors and tools.
Then we fools
Must get a machete
Or a bayonetti
To open bathroom stuff from Mennen,
And of course for Vladimir Lenin.

Planes and Cars

Sorry I missed the last meeting of the Lehigh Valley Region of the Antique Car Club of America. My wife and I were in Seattle attending the National Farm Bureau Convention. In addition to the trade show, we toured three farms. (You can take the boy off the farm but you can't take the farm out of the boy).

For me, the best part of the trip was the tour of the Boeing Facility. The factory building covers 94 acres and is the largest (by cubic feet) building in the world. The six rolling doors on the end are each as big as a football field standing on edge. We were allowed to walk on catwalks above its assembly line where the new 787 planes were being built. Major parts arrive just in time for assembly. Many are out-sourced and come from Taiwan, Japan and China. Parts come wrapped in plastic, like that which covers imported cars that come by boat. These huge sub-assemblies arrive by plane. Boeing has modified several 747's (the huge ones used for transoceanic flights), with a bigger, higher cargo area and a tail section that swings open to allow wing and fuselage sections to be air freighted to Seattle. Also on the tour was a visitor center with videos and details of the planes that are currently flying worldwide.

OK, dear reader, if you have stuck with me this far, you are probably wondering what in the world this has to do with antique cars. I'm coming to it now. There were cutaway jet engines on display at the visitor center, and just like at a car show I had to see what makes things go. There is a gear reduction inside jet engines, which reduces the very high speed of the turbines to enable them to drive the huge intake fans at the front of the engines. The gear reduction is a planetary gear set with a sun gear and planetary gears just like in Henry Ford's Model T transmissions that were first built 109 years ago. General Electric is also developing a two-speed reduction unit, but I am certain it will not be operated by foot pedals like the Model T Ford.

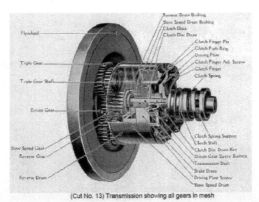

(Cut No. 13) Transmission showing all gears in mesh

Planetary transmission operated by foot pedals rather than by servos, solenoids or computers.

Drinking and Driving

Uncle Lou started out with a one-horse milk delivery wagon and built the business up to a modern creamery, employing over thirty men. He was, however, the original scrooge and never spent a cent. He brought his nephew into the company and, like many guys who worked in milk bottling plants, nephew Roy lived (or so they said), on hot steam and cold whiskey. Weston Sanitary Dairy made the very best Vanilla Bisque ice cream, and it was claimed that Roy even took an occasional nip of the vanilla extract.

In 1930, Roy inherited the business which was reported to be worth one million dollars. He bought some race horses, had a training track built for them at his buddy Charlie's farm and bought a new 1940 yellow Buick Century Convertible. Very soon, a horse threw him off. And he lost the convertible to Charlie in a card game. He immediately bought a 1941 Cadillac with hydramatic transmission because he had broken both his knees in the fall from the horse.

Roy also inherited Uncle Lou's office and kept a bottle of scotch in the oak roll-top desk but he wasn't just a closet drinker. He liked to go to the very best restaurants. One night, as he was leaving the Panache Club, he ran into a car in the parking lot. The early Hydramatics had a P N D L R shift pattern. The impact knocked the shifter into reverse with Roy's foot hard on the gas pedal. He tried to find the neutral but it got into low gear and rammed another car. The policeman on Third Street heard the crashes and came on the run. After hitting the fifth car, Roy found the key and managed to turn off the engine. With remarkable presence of mind, he produced an unopened bottle of Seagram's 7 from under the Cadillac's seat and gave it to the cop. He then went back into the club and announced, with considerable aplomb, that he had had a bit of an accident, would take care of all the damages himself and no one need bother calling their insurance company. The next week, he bought a total of six new cars.

And so it went on through the 1950's as the business gradually declined. Roy blamed it all on Lehigh Valley Dairy's competition with the new paper milk cartons and on the damage his plant suffered during the 1955 flood. By the 1960's, the plant was torn down, the site became a parking lot and Roy died in the County Poor House.

So if you inherit a million dollars, don't spend it all on cars - unless they are antiques!!

Teetotaler's Drink

I drink when dry or when I can,
Like every other working man.
Dogs do that as does the cat,
Drink when dry and that is that.
Before we call it a day,
We gotta unload two loads of hay.
No status nipple bottles for me, no siree.
I'd have to take time out to pee.
Like horses we work, then get food and water,
But I can't hold ten glasses like I oughter.
All my life I must have been dehydrated
Or like Pharaoh – desiccated.

MG, NOT OMG

Every old car has a story, some better than others. As of this writing, there is a 1935 High Wheel MG (1) four-seat touring car being restored by its owner in Mount Bethel, PA, which has a real story behind it.

Before World War II, it was owned by a lieutenant of the British Royal Navy (2). He was an aide to Winston Churchill who was, at that time, head of the royal navy. Churchill received a phone call that he was needed in London right away, but the train had left and the next scheduled two hours later.

What to do? The lieutenant offered to drive Churchill to London in his new speedy sports car. A photo exists of Churchill waving goodbye with his bowler hat in one hand and a cigar in the other.

After the war, the British naval lieutenant (which is a pretty high rank) sold the MG to an American naval lieutenant (a much lower rank). The American gave it to his British war bride who did not like the car (3). So, it rotted away in the briars. Perhaps we will get to see it restored to its previous regal glory.

(1) MG stands for Morris Garage.

(2) As in H.M.S. Pinafore.

(3) It wasn't her idea.

Mrs. Haas' School

I cried my first day of school. I was an only child, timid, bashful, and scared. Then I heard a contagious laugh and decided school might not be so bad after all: it was Russel Smith, and I had a lot of laughs with him until his untimely early death twenty years ago.

A one-room school is scoffed at by modern educators, but it worked well. Third and fourth-graders overheard what they learned in first and second, and fifth and sixth also got a refresher course. It worked the other way, too, with the smaller kids getting a jump on the next year. Big kids helped the small ones.

There was a big cast iron stove in the northeast corner, and one of the bigger kids came in early, took the coal ashes out behind the boys' outhouse, (1) and built up a new fire (2). One weekend, the fish bowl froze solid as did the goldfish. Both survived – bowl and all fish.

The county library truck came monthly and Mrs. Haas, our teacher, kindly informed me as to how the system worked, and that the books had to be returned. And that started my love for books and, I guess, this book, too.

(1) That is another story.
(2) Mrs. Haas probably paid him out of her own pocket.

Picture of Harry Frey (seated next to bike) and his cousin Esther Fair (center girl) and Harold Snyder (sitting next to Harry), circa 1914.

Mrs. Haas

Governmental agencies supplied "surplus commodities," and the Rooks and Ott kids were really poor and hungry. So, one winter some of the mothers came in to school and made tomato soup out of canned tomatoes, evaporated milk, dehydrated milk powder, and cistern water. The poor kids wolfed it down but would not eat the smelly sharp cheese which I loved. But we all were poor during the 1930-1938 Depression and did not know it.

Eventually all good things must come to an end. When the slats came off the belfry, pigeons moved in and used the slate roof to do their business. The county school superintendent came one day and figured out that the pigeon poop washed down to the rainspouts which emptied into the cistern from which our drinking water came (1). Much discussion ensued among the superintendent and Mrs. Haas: it was decided that there was no room for us in another school, so we should continue the school year in Carpentersville and get our drinking water from the nearby spring.

So every forenoon, Russel Smith and I hiked down to the spring and filled the galvanized Gott (2) cooler with fresh spring water and – like Jack and Jill – carried water up the hill to school. What Russel and I knew - and Mrs. Haas and the county superintendent did not know - was that every night Mr. Snyder kept his cows in the field where the artesian spring was and where the nice water cress grew.

Eventually the authorities figured it out, closed the school, transferred us to the big two-room Springtown School, and we never saw nice Mrs. Haas again. (3)

(1)   I always wondered what school superintendents did, and after serving 27 years on the local school board (1970-1997) I still don't know.

(2)   Galvanized metal is treated with lead to prevent rust. Gott now makes plastic water coolers.

(3)   Forty years later, we had a reunion of her students (with no tenure system back then, she had taught in at least four schools in Warren County), and she remembered everybody.

Spring with water cress and school in the background, 2017.

Mrs. Haas, (back row on the far right), with one of her classes outside the one-room Carpentersville School. Below shows the schoolhouse as it appears in 2017. See story on next page.

The School Still Stands in Carpentersville

Refurbished, repainted and stabilized for the future. The only things missing are the front steps, outhouses and the kids. Eight grades for both my father and me.

These one-room schools were not bad institutions. In point, the K-7 (eighth grade went to Shimer School, a Depression Era project). Classes were divided into K-1-2 grades, 3-4-5th grades and 6 – 7th grades. Thus, by the time students graduated, they had been exposed to the same lessons at least three times. Of course, kids were supposed to be doing their homework, but they could not help over hearing what the teacher was telling the other grades. The older kids could and did help the younger ones and acted as unpaid teachers. They thus helped to establish their own self-worth. When your homework was done you could read books from the book shelves, a virtual media center although somewhat dusty.

In winter, the school was heated by a big pot belly coal stove covered with a tin shroud to keep kids from burning themselves as they huddled around it to keep warm. One morning the goldfish bowl was frozen solid with the fish inside. To our amazement the fish and bowl survived. Flowers blooming and tadpoles growing were spring science projects every year.

The fire was tended by one of the big boys (7th graders) before, during and after school. This included bringing in kindling and taking the ashes out behind the outhouse.

This was during WWII and when a substitute teacher tried to ration us to one piece of toilet paper per day - it caused a minor rebellion. Nine-year old's creative thinking – the WPA built outhouse featured a chimney vent and sliding windows= cab windows + two wooden seats. Pecking order soon got shook out as to who was leader and peace prevailed. No bullies. No class distinctions, because we all were poor. Two WPA toilets outback. No guns but rabbit season guns were A- OK. We all carried knives.

Recess was the best time of all. Football (boys only), marbles, kickball. Antony over the schoolhouse roof,[1] motorcycle races on foot with sticks for handlebars, wrestling were all spontaneous.

Two of the big boys were engineer and fireman. The former wore his striped cap and hung his head out of the sliding vent window of the outhouse. Yanking on a string and hollering "Whooo whooo". The fireman was busy shoveling coal ashes from the ash pile into the toilet hole. The conductor 'loaded' the rest of boys and girls. The brakeman coupled up a hand to hand 'consist' (creative out of box thinking). One day one of the little kids barged into the locomotive cab and said he had to "go" - bad. The engineer and a fireman adamantly insisted this was their train and to go away. Instead he immediately lowered his drawers and left a really smelly deposit in the corner. Crew jumped from cab and that was end of Carpentersville and Southern Railroad for a while.

[1] Somewhat universal game of throwing a ball (Antony) over the schoolhouse roof.

Breakfast of Champions

Everybody knows what you are referring to when you say "Micky Dee's," but how many remember "Ho John's?" That was the nickname for a restaurant chain called Howard Johnsons which all had bright orange roofs and featured shredded and baked clam strips.

I will never forget the name Howard Johnson since we had a hired man by that name. It was during World War II, and help was impossible to find. Today, he would have qualified for disability payment and supplemental social security- but this was back then.

I was in grade school at the time, and I really don't know what the arrangements were, but Howard roomed at my grandparents' home and took his meal at my parents'. Perhaps he just worked for his room and board. At any rate, he lightened the load somewhat for my 70-year-old grandfather and my 40-year-old father. And he did work as best as he could, tending the horses and garden, and keeping things swept up.

He had a few disabilities: he had a wooden leg, superfluous fingers on each hand and supposedly an extra toe. (1) He was also prone to epileptic seizures. One morning, while we were all seated at my mother's kitchen table and eating cereal, he had a "spell" and barfed Wheaties all over Mom's kitchen table. (2)

When corn-planting time came, my father asked Howard to ride on the planter seat and raise and lower it at the end of each row, so my father "Harry" would not have to get off and then back on the tractor.

It all worked well, however Howard did eat a lot of dust kicked up by the tractor wheels. But while going up a hill diagonally at 5 5/8 miles an hour and the John Deere Model A Tractor wide open at 975 rpm, the planter runners hit a limestone outcropping, upset the planter, and threw Howard off. He landed like a chicken coming down out of a tree, got up, hobbled off, and he was never seen again. The Howard Johnson franchises no longer exist, but I will never forget that name.

(1) As a kid, I knew all about superfluous teats on a cow, but extra digits baffled me.
(2) I have never eaten Wheaties since that time.

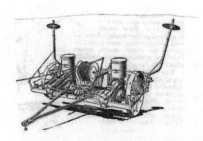

The Plymouth

I always liked the Rogers and Hammerstein's song "Some Enchanted Evening, You Will Meet a Stranger." That's the way I met my wife, Trudy. Bright, witty, college degree, good job, my age, and brand-new car. Couldn't go wrong. I've been accused of the fact that the 1956 Plymouth Belvidere was what caught my interest, but I deny it still today. Every romance has a story as does every car: over the years, that green sedan variously served as her commuter car, our kids' shuttle bus, my errand car, and occasional loaner. And Toots the First, our cat, had kittens under the front seat.

Story #1: The Agway truck broke down at my place, so I loaned that car to its driver to go get help. So, Will Apgar decided to take the Interstate back to the Agway plant; and when he felt a draft, he realized that he could see Route 78 down through the floorboards. So, he slowed down - way down. After a few miles, he saw flashing red and white lights in the mirror. A state policeman pulled him over and asked him why he was going so slow, to which he replied, "I am afraid to go any faster!"

Story #2: In 1972, my wife's niece wrecked her husband's new Corvette while he was an air force pilot flying C5A's out of Ft. Dix. It was their only car, so we offered them the Plymouth. Cars do fall victim to oxidation, and the Plymouth was no exception. Rust hit hard: the headlight eyebrows and the floorboards rusted out first. One rainy night there was some kind of fancy ball at the officers' club. Don't know if you've never been at an officers' club, but I would say that one would compare it to the fanciest inn. Pretty fancy fancy.

After the dinner dance, the niece's husband went for the car and pulled up under the marque to pick up his wife right alongside the general's big Lincoln, much to the delight of his buddies.

At one point, rust got to the brake lines, too, and my wife had brakes go out. (Reminder: check under your antique since cars before 1960 didn't have dual brake systems). She managed to get to a friend's house safely which was really further away than home, (with her two sons huddled down on the floor between the front and rear seats) and then I got the brake lines fixed.

Eventually, we parked the Plymouth. Birds pooped on it, weeds grew up around and under it, and the tires sank into the ground. Newton was right. In 1955, we planned a 100th anniversary of Great-grandfather Isaac moving to this farm – complete with party for all our friends and a square dance band. As you know, my party required getting ready and one priority was to get rid of all the junk, and the Plymouth was high on the list. I reluctantly called "Big Moose" the junk man and forgot all about the car. About two months later, I was on Interstate 78 and saw a trailer-load of compacted cars headed to Bethlehem Steel's open hearth, and right there in the middle of the load was a big turquoise cube. And I smiled a sad smile because a portion of my life was gone, gone forever.

CARL

Carl was a semi-retired farmer (1) who had rented out his fields and dispersed his dairy herd. He did keep a few brood cows. One of his Herefords expelled her uterus after calving (2). He called my son Bruce, the local large animal veterinarian. They took the cow outside, in case she died, and tied her to a fence post. Bruce disinfected things as best he could and worked to put the cow back together, only to have the cow push the uterus back out.

 Carl decided to help push things back in when his defibrillator went off, giving him a shock, the cow a shock, and Bruce a shock. Bruce then said, "Carl, you go sit on that hay bale. I can do this alone. But I can't deal with you dying!"

(1) He had a bad heart.
(2) A cow's uterus is about the size of a 10-gallon milk can and requires Herculean efforts to put back in the cow, since it weighs 100 lbs. and has the consistency of bloody canvas. It is like putting a rubber chicken into a wine bottle, only 100 times worse since the cow is constantly straining to expel it.

It Ain't Necessarily So

The holidays are over, and it's 2017 - a brand new year with new resolutions and hopes that everything will be better… But, as in the *Porgy and Bess* musical, "It ain't necessarily so."

The brand new 2017 cars are out and have been for months. (1) The new models always debut in late summer. This dates back to when ours was still an agrarian society and the farmers could first see the new models at the county fair. After wheat harvest was over, the farmer usually had some money by early fall. Thirty acres of wheat at twenty bushels each would buy a pretty nice car. Today, thirty acres of wheat at fifty bushels per acre times four dollars and thirty-five cents per bushel won't even buy a five-year-old used car. So much for parity!

A Model A Ford had a four cylinder engine, got 20 miles per gallon, had bucket seats and floor shift. When you opened the doors in a rainstorm the seat didn't get wet, and it was easy to get in and out. The bumpers were spring steel and would withstand a five-mph bump.

Ford soon went to a V-8 engine and by 1939, Chevrolet came out with 'fingertip' shift, which removed the gear shift from the floor and gave more leg room.

Ten years later, cars would seat three people comfortably in the soft front seat, and your girlfriend could - if she chose to - sit up real close to you.

In the 1970's, the four-cylinder foreign cars quickly responded to the oil embargo by becoming 'luxury' cars, with greatly increased prices. American manufacturers eventually responded by 'downsizing' and using the smaller chassis and motors from Falcons and Nova's and calling these luxury cars.

Front wheel drive designs (remember the Morris Mini) provided lighter weight cars and greater economy as domestic manufacturers changed back to four cylinders. Front-wheel drive and motors mounted crosswise would have eliminated any hump in front, but Madison Avenue decided bucket seats and floor shift, with a big console (plastic hump) between the front seats, would sell cars. Today, girlfriends can't sit up close - but can choose, "Your place or mine?" Bumpers will again withstand five mph crash tests but doors now dump rain and snow on the front seat when opened. Furthermore, 2017 Cadillacs have four-cylinder engines and eight speed transmissions – Oh, such progress!

So, here in the mid 2010's we're about back to where we started. If you live long enough, everything comes back. Like Einstein, I pondered time and space being a circle. But, eventually, I've decided time is like a corkscrew—you come back to right where you started—ALMOST!!

(1) Whoopie - 2017 cars have an advertising gimmick - a push-button ignition…which is what my 1950 Oldsmobile had. So much for progress.

Chicken Soup

About 25 years ago, our car club visited a then-new, million bird chicken farm. It was a very efficient operation with ingredients purchased in bulk and processed in their own feed mill. This was designed to produce a maximum number of hen fruit. When the chickens stopped laying eggs, they became Campbell's Mm Mm Good soup.

Ninety years ago, the Jacoby's had a very efficient chicken farm too with ingredients purchased wholesale and processed in their own feed mill. They also had the local school bus contract. When the chickens stopped laying, the Jacoby's turned them out to pasture with old, worn out school buses being used as shelters. Of course, the bus wheels, engines and seat bottoms had been removed first. These pullets would eventually start to lay eggs again and thus were saved from the stew pot temporarily.

The bus contracts that the Jacoby's had involved hauling the country kids to the high school in town. They also used the school buses to deliver eggs to various stores in the area and frequently had a crate of eggs next to the driver and just behind the gear shift lever. The town kids knew all of this and were just regaled with laughter over it. They called the girls chicks and old hens and the boys roosters and worse yet, capons and the bus was a chicken coop.

The bus I rode on, was a 1933 Chevy, one and one-half ton chassis with a wooden body. Jacoby usually replaced buses every eight or nine years but with WWII, new ones were not available. The bus was thus older than most of the kids in the high school. To say that the town kids "dissed" * us country kids is an understatement. Today's kids shoot each other over lesser taunts. Mr. Fretz was Jacoby's "right hand" hired man and drove our bus. He had a hearing aid the size of a walnut which he promptly turned off when the kids got on the bus, but he watched them in the mirror. There were a lot of bad roads in the country. In the winter of 1947, we had a snow storm and our bus got stuck. Back then, we went to school every day, snow or not. Mr. Fretz made all the boys get out of the bus to push, but when they got behind the bus and out of sight of the driver's mirror, the boys held back instead of pushing. Mr. Fretz had to get out and put chains on the 32/6-inch tires. If you've ever tried to put on truck chains while stuck in the snow bank, you'll know what he went through. The girls felt sorry for him and scolded the boys, who then did help the man get the bus going again, and off we went to school an hour late in the driving snowstorm.

A cold, wet and shivering Mr. Fretz stomped into the school with us and told the principal how bad the storm was. The principal promptly closed school and sent us all home on the bus. Hooray - the original snow day. The town kids, however, had to walk home in the snow and as we rode past them we got our long-awaited, sweet revenge and we had a happy winter holiday.

*Rap talk for being disrespectful toward someone else.

Brass to Cash

Farms tend to collect a lot of junk. Broken machinery and its pieces do pile up. We missed the high prices of scrap 14 months ago. But prices came back up some and the junk pile got even higher, so we sold several pickup loads of mixed iron.

There also was a big brass water tank that my father-in-law had in his greenhouse, and it brought $265 of green cash money. This came in handy on the geezer tour that my wife and I recently took to Utah, Nevada and California.

The high point of the trip for me was the Kennecott Copper Mine. It is the world's largest open pit mine and is visible from outer space. It is located in a six-thousand-foot-high mountain and is a mile across and a mile deep. The huge Caterpillar diesel electric trucks look like ants down in the bottom, as they crawl up the steep, spiral road, going around and around to get to the surface where each 250-ton load gets dumped into an equally huge crusher. The resulting slurry is then pumped nineteen miles to the refinery at the south end of Utah's Great Salt Lake.

Rio Tinto Corporation owns Kennecott Copper and other mines in South America and is supposed to be the world's largest supplier of copper. Since copper is used in almost everything electrical, it might be a very good hedge against the declining value of America's paper dollar.

Bob Frey's mailboxes – See story on next page.

Just Too Big

People seldom take Sunday drives anymore but on a bright sunny Sunday afternoon in March, somebody drove slowly by our farm in a shiny, red Falcon convertible with big chrome carburetors sticking out of the hood. They waved, then stopped and stared at our mail boxes. So, what is so special about mail boxes? If you've seen one you've seen 'em' all. Right? Well, not quite, since ours have some Franklin Mint model cars, J.B. welded on top and a forest green '51 Chevy pickup tailboard fastened underneath. As the late (great) Paul Harvey used to say, "and now for the rest of the story."

I had a roller bearing go out on a needed piece of farm machinery, and the new bearing fit loose. So, I went to the local branch of a famous nut and bolt franchise store for a tube of Loctite bearing mount. Guy says, "I'll have it overnight." That was Thursday. Friday, nope/ Saturday, closed/ Sunday, closed/ Monday, nothing/ Tuesday, nada/Wednesday, nada/ Thursday nut and bolt man called, 'It's unavailable." Somewhat angry, I jumped into my '51 Chevy pickup and promptly backed into a big farm wagon/tailboard, dead center. Went to Easton bearing store, guy says, "How many you want?" More disgusted, I told N&B store that they did not need my business. I somehow had a credit there and I wanted my money, "No can do." BIG company/must write for refund/ second letter return receipt/eventually got $200 check from N&B.

Take check to local branch of too-big-to-fail bank which I will call 2B2F. Girl at drive in window says, 'I can't cash this check." "Waddaya mean, you can't cash my check? I've had an account in this building for 40 years!" "You will have to come around to the main lobby." I parked my truck and stomped into lobby/immediately confronted by 2B2F bank Haus Frau/she tells me a company check must go into a business account. I say "I hain't got no business account - just a checking account that pays absolutely no interest."/ she says, "It's got a farm name on it"/ I say, "That's me, I am it, it is me!" The tellers and customers look on bemused/ I say, 'What about a payroll check, that's a company check?" She threatens to call cops/ I say, "How much money in that account?" They look at crystal ball/ I say, Good-gimme $10,000 in hundreds right now!"/ Haus Frau says," I can't do that."/ I say, "Why not? Where did my money go? Did it go 'poof' into derivatives and disappear?" Haus Frau says, "It is a 2B2F bank policy." I say, "We have stock in 2B2F and it's a shame you treat stock holders and customers like this!" Haus Frau says, "I will have my supervisor call you!" but they never called.

So, I fastened my old tailboard to our mailbox posts as a reminder of a couple of fun days and what it is like to deal with Big Business and banks that are too big to fail.

PS: I got my $10,000 the next day. Fresh from Obama's printing press.

Tony Pip

Phillipsburg was a busy industrial and rail center in the 19th and 20th centuries. Right in the center of things were Center and Green Streets (no pun intended). Ingersoll Rand and the associated Cameron Pump Company employed around three thousand locals. Many of their workers walked to work, but most drove and of course their cars would need tires, and 'Tony Pip' had a Kelly Tire franchise right at the workers' main entrance. Before radial tires were available, bias ply tires were only good for 20 thousand miles, and Tony Piperato did a thriving business recapping tires with what were locally known as "Tony Treads". People would leave their cars and walk to work and later in the day pick them up with their old tires wearing new treads. Workmen would buff off the old tread, apply glue and a thick rubber belt, and cook (vulcanize) the old tire in a mold, and presto! New rubber tread, good for another 20,000 miles.

It was hot, heavy and dirty work. Tony recapped big truck tires also and by the end of each day, his workmen were covered with rubber dust so that only their teeth and eye balls shown through. He treated his workmen just terribly, with a constant barrage of profanity in both English and Italian. People in the office waiting room would just cringe, and I even walked out once when Tony threw a tantrum at his hired help. But his workmen stayed with him for years. If ever there was a case of verbal harassment, it was at Center and Green Street, Phillipsburg.

Despite this, Tony was busy. You needed tires – Tony sold tires. His prices were low - low enough to beat all competition and low enough that customers would overlook Tony's harsh words and harsh treatment of employees. Also, Tony was related to half of the Italians in town and his wife/office girl "Skip" was related to half of the English. Furthermore, he knew everybody's last name.

Tony was a fan of high school sports, and he generously advertised in their event catalogs. He was an original "good old boy" and he made money. The epitome of first generation Italian immigrants. He and "Skip" liked to occasionally dine out at the most expensive restaurants, but he lived quite simply. What he did do was buy up properties in town as they came up for sale. And every ten years, he bought a new luxury car. Of course, he did not trade in the old one. He parked it out back of the tire store. Nothing is forever, and Tony passed away. A niece and nephew became executors and had to deal with all the properties Tony owned and with the auction. Club member Art Hawk bought and restored Tony's old 1960 Cadillac and is working on Tony's 1954 Chevy panel truck. His memory lingers on yet today, when somebody mentions Tony Pip, and knee-slapping tales are told at our cruise nights. Ah, to be remembered when you are gone.

Who Listens Better- Children or Adults?

It was a dark and rainy Halloween night as the members gathered in the Forks' Laneco parking lot. Woody Smith led us to the Binney and Smith Factory for our tour. As usual, some of us almost got lost, but all twenty-five finally showed up.

Our guides greeted us cordially and ushered us into a room with grade-school sized seats. They showed us a video of the Crayola crayon manufacturing and then started the actual tour of the factory. Just like the school groups, we were warned to stay behind the yellow lines and obey the guide.

They showed us how paraffin and pigments are heated, mixed and poured into molds. This is done both by hand and by highly sophisticated pneumatically activated machinery. The crayons are then automatically wrapped and stored in wooden boxes until needed by the machinery which automatically packages the crayons in 8, 16, 32, 64 or 96 crayon boxes for world-wide distribution.

As the tour ended, Glen Snyder wandered through an open, automatically operated overhead garage door which promptly came down and just barely missed him. (He didn't stay behind the yellow lines). The guide was a little upset by this and also made a point of warning Jack Miller not to write on walls with his sample crayons. I guess antique car people are an awful lot like grade school kids!!

Our group was the very last to have an evening tour of the factory, since Binney and Smith and their parent company (Hallmark cards) have started work on a Hershey-type visitor center in Easton in hopes that it will help to rejuvenate the downtown.

We applaud Binney and Smith for being concerned with the community- for employing 1200 local people instead of making their crayons some place in China. We commend them for this, and we thank Woody for giving us the opportunity to tour their actual facility.

(Note: in 2017 Crayola dropped the color yellow and invented a new blue. How will kids now color the sun in the new blue sky?)

Wheels

It is believed by some that the early Mezzo Americans knew about the wheel but did not utilize it because they knew it would cause trouble down the road (no pun intended).

Thus it was that my bride of fifty years and I would be waiting at the airport in a foreign country, where we could not speak a word of the language and our contact person could not be found. Fortunately, Trudy was originally a city girl and knew (was familiar with) about rail travel, and the people of the Netherlands are most kind and helpful. After a twenty Euro ride (that's $27 US money) in a diesel Mercedes taxi and two train rides, we found our friend "Chris". But, for a while we were two (old) babes in the woods, two lost souls... confused elderly couple.

Now back to the wheel. Some years ago, I saw a "wanted" ad in the *Vintage Truck* magazine for a steering wheel for a 1946 Ford truck. I had blown the engine in my flathead V8 one and one-half ton from hauling five tons of red shale. I was planning to scrap it, so I answered the ad. I tried to pull the steering wheel off, but 50 years of rust was too much, so I took it off with my thermal wrench, packed it up and sent it to the Netherlands.

That recipient came walking in one October day (Hershey week) and we became friends (albeit with a bit of a language problem) with a common interest in old iron. He was back in the states last fall, and I took him to "America on Wheels" and to the rusted remains of Bethlehem Steel now known as Steel Stacks.

When Trudy and I signed up for a grand (farm) tour of Europe one summer which started in Amsterdam, we wrote to Chris. He was to meet us at the airport there. When we borrowed a cell phone from a nice Dutch lady and contacted Chris he said, "Oh was that today?" But it worked out fine, and Chris took us to see his own private large museum of cars, trucks and European military vehicles. Chris had the garbage contract for the city of Den Hang – a town the size of Bethlehem, PA, sold it and started collecting vintage wheels. We still correspond.

Chris (on right) and his truck with my steering wheel.

Flip Flops

Warm weather and women are wearing flip flops again. Car nuts are familiar with the expensive "flip-flop" metallic paint jobs sported on some hot rods. Depending on which way the sunlight hits the vehicle, it appears to change from copper, to bronze, to pink, maroon or purple shades and thus called flip-flops.

We had a tom cat we called Flip-flop. I can't remember whether he was born on the farm, was dropped off, or just wandered in from the neighbor's place. He was dirty white with gray spots. His head was twisted a quarter-turn to the left, and he walked like the proverbial drunken sailor. Also, his rear legs did not track behind his front legs, much like a truck with a broken shackle bolt. Dogs trot that way also. Flip-flop may have suffered from ear mites, which messed up his ear drums and caused him to lose his sense of balance so that he would sometimes stumble and fall over. However, he had an oversupply of testosterone and worked 24-7 chasing female cats and saying "Wow." I don't know that he ever scored, but he ran into a lot of other tomcats.

The resulting fights were even funnier than today's GEICO commercials. He was afraid of nothing and would attack any and all tomcats. He would stalk them as best he could and pounce, landing perhaps a foot away from the target. If the other cat ran Flip-flop would chase it at top speed, crashing into things. Usually a fight ensued with biting, scratching, clawing and balls of fur flying. The other tomcats were overwhelmed by his fighting style. He didn't bite where he was looking, so he bit in strange tender places. There would be handfuls of cat fur floating around in the wind. Not a day went by without a cat fight, and we would stop work to watch. I don't remember what happened to Flip-flop but for a time he was top cat. However, I recall no kittens that looked remotely like him.

OK dear reader, you've stuck with me this long, so I will finally get to the point. My wife and I took a creative writing course in Brasstown, NC at the John C. Campbell Folk School. Back in the 1920's, the wealthy Campbell family (not the soup people) set up a live-in school to educate the ignorant hillbillies in the region, teaching modern farming, proper cooking measures and ways to profit from home industries such as quilting, hooked rugs, blacksmithing, basket making and making and playing mountain dulcimers. Now they teach these crafts to an increasing affluent urban public. The Smoky Mountain Campbell School has really flip-flopped.

Souders Brothers

In the summer of '42', the Mills Brothers were popular and so were the Souders brothers. Mr. Souders senior had a family creamery business, processing and selling milk door to door. He had two handsome sons whom he loved dearly and when WWII broke out, he bought them a farm. He then convinced the draft board that Uncle Sam needed his boys to produce the milk to supply the creamery which supplied the milk for the town whose workers supplied canisters for 50mm shells and toilet seats.

The sons knew nothing about farming but read up on it in *Successful Farming* magazine. With Daddy writing the checks and his connections with the Ration Board, they got a new Allis Chalmer Crawler Model S tractor, a John Deere Model 100-disc plow and a Killifer cultivator of the type shown in magazines. They also got a 550-gallon fuel tank, as that big Allis Chalmers 5 ¾ x 6 ½ four-cylinder engine liked its gas.

It's pretty hard to cultivate corn with a crawler type tractor, but the boys found it was easy to attract girls. The word soon got out that here were two good looking guys who were not in the Army, were not classified 4-F, were "batching it" in an eight-room Victorian house back a long lane, and...who had lots of free gasoline.

Jim left the tractor idling for hours once while he went joyriding with a car-load of girls. It was reputed that Tom even left the milking machines sucking on the last two cows all night long. Mrs. Crouse also claimed to have seen girls leaving the Souders farm when she went out to her barn at 5:30 am. Ah, what great delicious gossip!

When the war was over and the brave servicemen came home, everyone figured that the Souders would sell the farm...but no, instead the boys bought a white M.G. TC high wheel roadster and took turns with it. One night, Tom used it and the next it was Jim's turn to pick up girls. They also took turns with the farm work (sort of). By 1948, they traded the M.G. in for a new red Jaguar 120 XKE roadster and reached new heights of popularity.

But all good things must come to an end, and when Jim and some girl took off (with the Jag) for Florida, it was just too much for Tom. He sold the farm - lock, stock and barrel - and the neighbors had to find somebody else to gossip about.

The Buggers

Dear Albina,

I must apologize for not writing sooner. Hopefully, the man will smuggle this out and mail it. I paid him enough so he should! Trudy and I are in separate sections but do see each other daily. We do a lot of reading, watch some TV and of course, we exercise.

It all started early last Labor Day when we decided to take the Model T Ford for a spin. We removed the flannel car cover, dusted it off with the Kozak rag, pumped up the tires, checked the oil spigot, put in some fresh lawn mower gasoline, turned the gas shut-off to 'on' position, jacked up the right rear wheel and made sure the other three wheels were blocked front and rear. I filled the radiator with hot water, released the emergency brake, retarded the spark, opened the throttle one third, turned the ignition key to 'battery', cranked it over twice, and it started right up! I switched the key to 'magneto', advanced the spark, slowly pulled the emergency brake on, lowered the right rear wheel to the ground, and the engine settled right down to an even idle. I removed the wheel chocks, and we climbed in and headed down Creek Road to River Road. It was just like old times, touring in an open Model T...mountains on one side and winding river on the other.

And then we heard it - a deep "whomp, whomp, whomp, whomp" noise. Oh damn! It's a main bearing going out. After eighty years a bearing has to go out and we are twenty miles from home. "Damn, Damn, Damn!!" I slowed down, but still the noise continued at the same rate. I retarded the spark and opened the throttle but the noise continued at the same rate. Whomp, whomp, whomp and THEN the voice over the loud speaker said, "You in the blue car, pull over, get out, face the car, put hands on the roof and spread your legs apart!!!"

We hurriedly did so as the helicopter landed. Four armed SWAT Team members dressed in black surrounded the car and frisked us. Then one of the men, the one with the jodhpurs, black leggings and riding crop, went back to the helicopter and got a thing that looked like an old Electrolux vacuum cleaner, complete with a long hose which he stuck up the exhaust pipe of the Model T. The view screen reeled off numbers like a digital gas pump, a buzzer sounded, and the device spat out a two-foot long printout.

The one in charge looked at the printout, read us our rights under the Miranda Act and then informed us that our car was in violation of seven items under the new Environmental Disaster Act as passed by Congress and signed by President Gore. The car did not have a catalytic converter, had not been dynamometer tested, wasn't burning oxygenated fuel and was off the scale in CO, SO_2, NO_2 and a whole bunch of other evil items. Just then the wrecker and squad car arrived. They stuck an orange hazardous waste sign on the Model T with orders to the wrecker driver that the car be compacted immediately and the mandatory verification form (in quadruplicate) be sent to the proper authorities by registered mail.

(Continued on next page)

The Buggers – *(continued)*

They hooked the Model T to the wrecker and took it away. They put us in the police car and took us away—in handcuffs. Our lawyer says he will try to get us off as being INCOMPETENT.

If only we hadn't trusted the politicians back in 1996-97 when they said antique cars would be exempt from pollution control laws. They changed the law on us when we let down our guard. I guess this just proves that the politicians tell us what they think we want to hear and then do as they please... THE BUGGERS!!

Oh yes, Albina don't forget to send the Antique Car Club newsletter to us now at the county jail.

PS: Albina Morris was the editor of our Antique Car Club newsletter and the one who asked me to write a monthly column from which these stories were picked.

Frey's 1917 Model T Ford #1922575, built June 1917

1926 Model T Ford Huckster Truck

We run across stories like this frequently in the AACA magazine, in *Hemmings*, and in other old car publications. Somebody finds an antique car hidden away in an old barn which hasn't seen daylight in years. People occasionally get a glimpse of a Model T doodle bug in my wagon house, and they stop and find an eccentric old farmer who will not part with his treasure.

I recently got involved in the rediscovery of a 1926 Model T Ford Huckster Truck. I had heard about its existence for years. I got a call from "Hank Junior" who was finally considering selling it to an acquaintance we will call "Ben". The Ford was in Hank's late uncle's two-story frame blacksmith shop. The structure had been placed on the National Historic Registry and had a plaque to prove it. Actually, the whole hamlet had been placed on the Historic Registry in a futile attempt to stop a new big box super store from coming in.

The key fit the lock and the door creaked open and we peered into the blackness. It soon became obvious that we had to remove both parts of a forty-foot extension ladder to get inside. Then we were confronted with boxes of glass Mason jars, Planet Junior garden tools, boxes, milk crates, chicken crates, a crumbling forge, anvils, tongs, hammers, fishing rods, eel gigs, piles of empty potato sacks and stuff I did not recognize. All of this detritus of several lifetimes was once somebody's treasure and we had to climb over and through it.

As we examined the truck, Hank related its history to us. It was purchased new by the town fire company as a ladder truck and was equipped with a Ruckstell 2-speed rear. Some of the gilded lettering still showed through the dust. Eventually, Hank's uncle bought it and used it as a huckster truck to deliver his home-grown produce to town.

Every Saturday morning, he would pick up Hank and head for the city, where Hank would go door to door with a basket of vegetables and ask each housewife if she needed anything. When they finally sold all the produce, Hank's uncle would stop at a tiny restaurant and buy Hank a ham and cheese sandwich and a five-cent bottle of soda pop.

The hood and doors opened easily but the engine was stuck tight. Standing on the crank handle only threatened to bend the crank. So we sprayed the spark plug holes with WD-40 and reluctantly left the Model T where it was so Ben could think about whether it would make a good rolling billboard for his small family business.

We picked our way back through the junk, put the extension ladders back inside and locked up the building. We all decided it would take 3 or 4 guys at least 3 full days to get the Model T out into daylight. There was some doubt as to whether Ben really wanted the Model T truck, and there was also some doubt if Hank really would sell it, in as much as he never got rid of anything. Hank's 43-year-old daughter would like to see things sold now so that she doesn't have to dispose of his estate. Of course, at 84 years old, Hank is not thinking about dying because he has a new 38-year-old wife. Any resemblance here to persons living or dead is purely coincidental.   (PS: Hank's young wife ran off with all his money.)

WHOA

Some time ago, I wrote about Horace who invented his very own cow barn manure conveyor system which was copied by, patented by and sold by a large (James) equipment company. Horace never got one cent.

Horace had a brother who was equally clever. In the late 1930's, Clayton farmed on the edge of a small town, actually it might be better called a village as there were at best 60 houses, two churches, one undertaker (that's another story), a couple of mom and pop stores and a railroad siding. There also was a post office and two lodge halls - the Odd Fellows and the Grange Hall.

The National Grange was founded after the Civil War to help resolve the animosities between the north and south and to organize rural people for their own and their community's betterment. Local meetings were held twice monthly with a certain amount of ritual work but stressing lectures, debates, and issues that affected rural folks. Local charities were supported by money from sausage and pancake suppers, refreshment stands at farm sales and square dances. A lot of country bumpkins (myself included) met their spouses at Grange Halls.

Clayton and his family belonged to the Grange. This, incidentally, was the first lodge that allowed women members and permitted them to become officers. The officers took their positions seriously, especially the Master. The secretary and the treasurer also acted as purchasing agents. Several times a year the officers would solicit orders for fertilizer and salt. Such supplies were cheaper for the members since the Grange acted as the distributing entity for the supplier and got a discount for carload lot purchases. Each member paid only his own share of the whole order. No commission was ever charged.

Clayton ordered his spring supply of fertilizer. Forty acres of corn at one hundred pounds per acre was two tons of 10-10-10. The railroad car arrived at the siding on the appointed day, and the members were telephoned to pick up their orders the next day since the railroad charged a demurrage fee after the third day.

Everybody arrived on time and started helping to unload the shipment. The younger men competed to see who was fastest and strongest and the officers counted the bags as they were unloaded (Where did the awful term 'Off" loaded ever come from?) and collected the money.

The farmers arrived in all sorts of conveyances. Mostly Chevy and Model TT Ford trucks and an occasional old sedan with the backend sawed off and made into a truck. Clayton arrived with a team of horses and a flat hay wagon. As I said, Clayton was clever and had sawed off the spokes and felloes and mounted 6.00X16 tires and wheels from a wrecked 1937 Ford car. He used the wagon hubs. I still can't figure out how he did it but he did it none the less. He deftly backed his team around so that the wagon was right up to the boxcar door. The men helped him load up his forty-one hundred-pound bags of fertilizer just as he had helped two

(*Continued on next page*)

WHOA *(continued)*

others load. It was hard work but a jolly good time was had by all.

Clayton headed home with his fertilizer. It was an easy load for the horses since the main street was on a very gentle slope on the same grade as the small brook which paralleled the road. It was slightly downhill all the way. Clayton had modified the wagon brake somehow to work against the rubber tires just like the famous Conestoga wagons of pioneer fame.

A block of oak rubbed on each rear tire when the driver actuated a brake lever at the front of the wagon. It worked fairly well, but the design was far from the self-energizing, modern disc brakes.

About halfway home, Clayton realized that the oak blocks were smoking, and the rubber tires were smoking, and the wagon was gaining ever so slowly on the horses that had been going along at a nice clip-clop. It was inevitable that the traces and the swivel tree would soon bump the horses' hocks, which would spook the horses to go faster and speed things up even more. Clayton decided he ought not to tell the horses 'Giddy yup', as that would also make matters worse. His best chance, he thought, would be to go right straight through the intersection and eventually get stopped outside of town in a meadow alongside the road. Hopefully, he wouldn't run into the brook.

But the horses had different ideas. They knew the way home. Home was where the hay was and that meant a 'hard right' turn at the intersection. The wagon spun out like a midget dirt track racer. Clayton let loose of the reins and held onto the headboard of the wagon for dear life and yelled to his 4-year-old son Jim: "Get to the back of the wagon!" The horses side-swiped the funeral parlor and ended up in a tangle of trace chains, harnesses, hame straps, hoofs, and horse flesh. Nobody got hurt, the horses recovered but the ancient cut limestone building on the southeast corner of the Stewartsville square still bears the scratch marks where that team of horses' side-swiped it all those years ago. It's right across the street from Stewartsville Grange Hall #121.

Glenny's Curiosity

Glenny liked to help his daddy, Glen. At the age of two and a half, he knew the difference between 7/16, 1/2, and 5/8-inch wrenches and would cheerfully fish them out of the toolbox and fetch them to 'old' Glen as needed. Glenny had his own little tool box and learned early on how to use screwdrivers and pliers to unbend the metal tabs that held his toy Tonka trucks together. He just loved to see how things were put together. Once, he "fixed" grandpa's windup alarm clock by taking the escapement out of it. When wound up, it made a nice whirring sound that was reminiscent of the cow clippers running. Glenny captured the family cat and ran his homemade "clippers" all over it and managed to get the cat's tail wound up in the gears. There was a lot of noise and excitement for a while.

Old Glen liked his eleven to seven shift because it was cooler in the mill at night and the schedule allowed him to fish, hunt and to work around the house in the daytime. It also allowed him more time to be with his family. One morning, he arrived home from work and his wife informed him that they did not have any water. He went down to the cellar, checked the fuses and found that the jet type pump would run but not pump. He got a pail of water and back in the cellar, he used a funnel and poured water into the priming hole with no success. He then coupled his garden hoses to his neighbor's outside faucet and ran the hose through his cellar window. He asked six-year-old Glenny to go next door and turn on the water. The pump absolutely would not pick up the prime. Dismayed, he got his pick and shovel and started to dig. The outside pipe to the well itself was below frost level, so he had to dig down four feet, all the way to the well casing itself. The pipe looked good with no wet spots, so he had to uncap the well and pull the drop pipe. Fortunately, Glen was strong and little Glenny helped also. Daddy sent junior inside for a mirror and was able to see that there was indeed water in the well. This was a big relief. He next examined the foot valve and found it was worn out and would not hold the water from running away.

Glen and Glenny jumped in his Ford 150 pickup and headed to the Sears store where he had bought the pump originally. They had a similar unit on the floor but would not sell the foot valve from it. They told him he would have to go to the Sears Repair parts depot in Allentown, PA. They found the place, got a number and awaited their turn. Glen, of course, had the model and serial numbers from the pump and the old valve in hand. The clerk looked into the Fisch crystal ball and said, "Pay now and we will have the part in a week to ten business days." Glen stalked out and headed for the new, big box depot store which was advertised as having everything for home owners. The associate in the plumbing department looked at the old part and asked, "What's this for? We don't have anything like that!" Then Glen tried a couple of mom 'n pop hardware stores to no avail but Mr. Miller of Miller's Hardware in Easton suggested that there was a plumbing supply store near Nazareth, PA. Glen handed the part to the counterman there who said, "How many do you want?" Glen paid cash and hurried home. His wife handed him a sandwich and he sat down for just a moment in the kitchen. He had a bad morning. Glenny was not in sight. Glen put the new valve on the drop pipe and without Glenny's help lowered it back down into the well. He then shoveled the dirt back into the ditch and stomped it all down. Glen went down to the cellar, primed the pump again and bingo- no water. He swore and checked the pump again, tried the water hose from next door and nothing. Zilch!

So, he dug the ditch again, pulled the pipe and was preparing to return the valve, when he realized the valve assembly didn't look just right. He took it apart and found the flapper was in backwards. "That's funny", he thought as he changed it around, put it together and installed the whole works back down in the well. This time, he tried the pump before he closed up the ditch and it worked. It was getting dark but he figured he should backfill the ditch so the kids would not fall into it. Then it hit him that he had not seen Glenny for hours. He found the boy on the sofa watching TV and looking guilty. Glenny had taken the new valve apart to see how it worked and put it back together wrong. Glen did make it back to work by 11 pm, and Glenny wasn't too popular for a few days. But father and son are the best of hunting and fishing buddies today, and Glenny is a top-notch mechanic with the State Department of Transportation.

* * * * * * *

CONFINED

Here I am in total captivity,
Isolated from my usual activity,
They tell me I'm sick.
Was it from that blasted deer tick?
Right now this hick
Would druther be up on a hay rick
In the boiling hot sun or hunting grundsow with my gun.
My mind gets muddled, at times befuddled.
A nurse, cute but sadistic,
Brings Dixie cups of plastic
Full of pills generic
Which I think have made me sick.
They are extruded through 100 mesh screens
Like jelly beans
In a limekiln in Bangladesh
That is my guess.

Cross-overs

I was waiting in line at an airport car rental desk, when an elderly man (probably younger than I am now) stormed in yelling, "That Buick has no back-seat room!" The rental girl clerk said, (and I kid you not) "What are you planning to do, pick up a lot of girls?" To her credit, the clerk did upgrade the old gent to a Cadillac and he was happy.

I understand that the 2017 Cadillac's have a four-cylinder engine and an eight-speed transmission, just the opposite from Cadillac's usual big V8 with a four-speed transmission. And, I bet the new Cadillac has less rear seat leg room than the 2017 biggest Chevrolet or a 1929 Model A Ford sedan, for that matter. The big ones are getting smaller and the small ones are getting bigger.

I remember laughing at the first imported Morris-Minis with tiny crossway motors and front wheel drive. Today almost every modern car has front wheel drive and Morris Minis are bigger than the smallest Chevys (or is it Cherrys)? BMW was a peppy small car and is now a luxury sedan and has its own big cross-over.

One night last September, five kids in a late model BMW failed to make a slight bend in the road by our farm, ran up the bank fifty yards, rolled over, took down one hundred feet of guard rail and did a half dozen upside down donuts on the macadam, and they all survived. There were air bags everywhere. The driver did disappear into our corn field but all were alive. New cars are definitely safer but I still like old cars that are strictly stock, (except for modern seat belts maybe).

But exactly what is a "cross-over" and how much did Detroit pay somebody to come up with that name? Maybe it has something to do with being politically correct (LGBT). Is a cross-over an Estate Wagon – 1916? A Suburban – 1936? A station wagon – 1946? A sports utility vehicle- 1986? The only difference that I can see is that cross-overs have a tin shelf over-hanging the rear window, which may or may not house a third taillight. Some of these extensions look like one third of a thick crust pizza.

The next thing the car industry comes up with may be tires with white sidewalls and fender feelers from circa 1947.

The Old Road to Perdition

The summer of 2002 brought forth a goodly number of so-called "Blockbuster" movies, most of which had no redeeming values other than a couple of hours in an air-conditioned theater for the movie goer.In my mind, there is one exception and it is entitled *The Road to Perdition*. It has a gangster plot, two male actors whose work I enjoy and (you guessed it) lots of antique cars. The story takes place in 1931, and there are many Model T and Model A Fords in the street scenes.

I remember when *The Dain Curse* movie was shot in Easton and in front of the Northampton County Courthouse. The production crew were most courteous to those of us who brought our Model T's, of course they could afford to be nice since they needed cars appropriate for the era. It was a great experience to see how movies are made and to eat at the same catered buffet as James Coburn. Scenes of my 1917 were limited to one shot of it parked along the retaining wall on Walnut Street. I got a check for $75 for the day, but I would have gladly paid $75 for the day's fun!

The late Harry and Albina Morris and their 1950 Chevy Sedan were in a movie 20 years ago, and the production company not only paid them but paid their screen actor guild dues and gave Albina a new old-fashioned hair-do also.

In *Road to Perdition* the scenes, the clothing and the autos are appropriate to the Depression Era. I certainly don't want to be considered one of the "correct police" but the 1931 Buick used by hit man Tom Hanks was the proper John Deere green, but the hood was all faded out like the car had been parked outside in the hot California sun in some Hollywood lot for the last forty years. After a shootout, the hero/villain brush-painted it the proper rich burgundy color that my neighbor's restored 1931 Buick Roadster is painted.

Paul Newman played an aging industrial-strength godfather, and there is no gushy romance anywhere in the plot...just stress on family and "family values" as defined by the Cosa Nostra which of course does include considerable shooting. Thus the 'R' rating. I rate it five stars, and it will must surely be available on Netflix. By all means, plan to see it.

PS: Perdition means eternal damnation - so says Webster.

* * * * * * *

Old 'Saint' Nick

In the days before television, my parents eagerly awaited their *Saturday Evening Post* magazine. My father liked the 'Earthworm Tractor' series; my mother enjoyed writings of James Thurber and poems by WW Watt.

Sometimes the *Post* wouldn't arrive until the following week - But Why? Complaints to the town postmaster brought only a shrug. Eventually, a family discussion revealed that Grandpa's *National Geographic* and Uncle Charlie's *Popular Mechanics* occasionally arrived late and somewhat dog-eared. They therefore concluded that Old Nick must read people's mail before he delivered it.

Old Nick did, indeed, know everybody's business on his rural free delivery mail route. He also loved nothing better than to stop to tell you that no matter what you were doing, he knew a better way to do it. He also liked to advise you that your garden was weedy or if there was one board off of your fence. His own place, which was once a Victorian showplace, was a bit of a disaster. There were shingles off the roof, the porch had fallen off leaving a big hole in the siding, and mock orange bushes and poison ivy surrounded the house.

But as the postal service proudly advertised, the mail always got through - although sometimes belatedly. His Model T Ford Coupe had a homemade box on the back, and every morning after milking his ten cows and eating a big breakfast, he would haul his two forty-quart cans of milk to the creamery, stop at the Post Office, pick up the mail and deliver it on his way home.

If it was snowing, he would stop at the GLF Feed Store and buy a couple of 100 lb. bags of wheat bran for added traction. Model T Fords had skinny tires, high clearance, only 20 horse power but lots of torque and his usually got him through the deepest snow. If the 'knobby' tires did spin, he would cuss and swear and wrap a couple of harness trace chains around the tires, snap them fast to the wire wheel spokes, and off he would go again with the chains flip-flopping against the fenders and knocking off a year's accumulation of mud.

Nick wore bib overalls and the same brown sweater, all covered with cow hair, for about nine months of the year. He wore his Woolworth eyeglasses on the end of his nose and always had a cigar in his mouth. He never smoked it - just chewed on it. He was a bit of a problem to the postal service because he would forget to cash his paychecks or lose them behind the seat of the Model T.

One afternoon, while he was doing his chores, a real estate developer wearing a gray flannel suit drove in with a brand-new silver gray Cadillac Sedan Deville, offered to buy Nick's farm to build five hundred houses on one-quarter-acre lots. Old Nick said, "No." The realtor upped the price as Nick figured out the new Cadillac cost as much as Nick had paid for his farm when he bought it in 1935 and that the guy's suit cost more than Nick's Model T was worth. Nick listened to the realtor as long as he could until he finally exploded with, "No! You just get the hell off of my

(Continued on next page)

Old 'Saint' Nick (*continued*)

place, and don't ever come back with your fancy-assed clothes. Don't you know, Sir, that there are more Important things in life than money?"

The word eventually got out and the neighbors "cluck-clucked" about crazy Nick turning down $150,000 for his run-down place and his saying that there are more important things in life than money. "IMAGINE THAT!" they said.

But forty-five years later, the trees and meadows there still green up every spring just in time for the bobolinks and vesper sparrows. The township did not have to build a new sewer plant or new school for the thousand extra kids or hire more police or build more access roads and maybe (just maybe) our contrary eccentric Old Nick was a Saint after all.

(See story on page 93 for more on hauling milk.)

Emerald Isle Green

Trudy and I spent twelve days in Ireland over a Labor Day weekend. Here are one farmer's observations.

They call it the Emerald Isle and green it is, but not the shade of green of our blue grass, orchard grass or brome. It is more the color of our grass if you cover it with a piece of plywood for a couple of days; thus the emerald name. The grass provides nourishment for twelve million cattle and millions of sheep. Four million people live there also, on an island somewhat larger than Pennsylvania. The glaciers dumped lots of rocks on Ireland, and for centuries the people have been picking them up and piling them in fence rows which surround the four- or five-acre fields for the cattle. The European Union has decided that Ireland should provide dairy products and meat for the rest of Europe. Barley and oats are grown on the most fertile land, and the combines are very modern. Surprisingly, farm tractors are allowed on the interstate-type highways and will do 40 mph, which is twice that of our domestic ones. Sheep are raised on the less fertile areas and up on the mountain sides. Peat is still dug by hand in the bogs. It is cut into hoagie roll-sized chunks, dried and then burned in fireplaces, giving off smoke and a nice earthy smell. Today most homes are heated with oil which comes from Libya. All the Irish television talking heads were in a dither about the Middle East.

Dublin is a very cosmopolitan city with many people on the streets just like New York City. It is a university (free tuition) town with lots of red-headed Bonnie Lasses in their black stockings and short-short skirts. Block-long row houses have identical facades, but each door is painted a different bright primary color. Houses in the small towns and in the country are made of stone or brick and painted in a thousand shades of pastel yellow.

Cathedrals and castles that were built of stone (obviously) a thousand years ago still stand. I really don't know how they built them. I did not feel the need to climb the 177 steps to hang upside down to kiss the Blarney Stone. Dublin appeared to be prosperous, with twenty people standing in the securities and investment line[1] at the AIB Bank where we exchanged $1.50 US dollars for each 1 Euro note. The plumbing in the hotels is, to say the least, unique. A smart feature is that the plastic hotel key card must be inserted in a slot other than the one to open the door to turn on the room lights. Hotel breakfasts were great and featured Canadian-style bacon (yum-yum), fried red tomatoes, two kinds of sausage, runny baked beans, eggs, potatoes, real oatmeal along with American-style cereals with real cream. Hotel meals included beef, mutton, chicken, cod and salmon, and are heavy with potatoes, carrots, rutabagas, artichokes, parsnips and spinach. Soups are excellent and are all pureed and look like mud. Desserts are fattening, and portions are large but the Irish people are not as obese as Americans. This may be because they use real sugar, not high fructose corn sweetener.

(*Continued on next page*)

Emerald Isle Green (*continued*)

Lots of Guinness and whiskey are brewed and consumed with four or five pubs on every city block.

Secondary road intersections all have roundabouts (small traffic circles) barely negotiable by large tour buses. Buses are more modern than those here, with more glass area. Although there is a limit to how streamlined a brick-shaped bus can get, they seem to have tried. Van Hool, Brockheer and other bus bodies are mounted on Volvo, Mercedes, Scania, Man and Iveco chassis. The heavy trucks are all cab over engine type and over the road trailers have three axles with 'fat cat' tires (no duals). Dump trucks dump all three ways. Cadillacs, Lincolns and pickup trucks are non-existent. Gasoline is 1.50 Euros per liter which figures out to be two American dollars a gallon more than it is here. Esso stations predominate. Remember the tiger in your tank? There are lots of small Fords, and every make of foreign car is found in Ireland, including some not seen here, such a Peugeot, Fiat, Skoda, Travat, Vauxhall and Citroen which incidentally are still as goofy looking as are the old Model 2 CV's. Almost all cars appeared to be less than five years old, and the only antique cars I saw in 1500 miles of bus travel were five old MG's on a tour and one 1922 Model TT truck. So, there is little else I can think of to write about except to say Ireland is a beautiful green country, and visiting it should be on everyone's bucket list.

[1] When have you last seen 20 Americans lined up to buy investments?

Eastern States Standard Oil Co., circa 1960

Driving Mrs. Daisy

Today there are people who do not know how to drive a car with manual shift, especially women. Fifty years ago, there were people who did not know how to drive period, especially women and Daisy was one of them. She lived on a ranch in Montana, and every two weeks her husband Will drove her 35 miles to town for supplies. The whole family went, so it was a major production. This was long before Walmarts were scattered in a grid across the country. People relied on the catalogs from Sears & Roebuck and Montgomery Ward, RFD mail delivery and their own gardens. They did not need to go to a store every single day.

One spring, the appointed Saturday arrived, and at breakfast Daisy told Will about what they needed to get in town that day. Will grunted and went out to the barn. After a while Daisy hunted him up and said they were all ready to go. Will said he couldn't go because it was going to rain and he needed to sow the oats and reseed the meadow or the horses wouldn't have anything to eat next winter. She said that she had to go to town or they wouldn't have anything to eat next winter. He said he had plowed, disked, harrowed and picked rocks all week. Jake had loaned them his grain drill and wanted it back tomorrow. Will finally said, "I can't go to town. I won't go to town and that's all there is to it. I don't want to hear any more about it. If you want to go to town, woman, there is the Jeep. Go to town, dammit!" The kids stood a safe distance away and watched in silence as Daisy reddened, turned on her heel and went into the house.

She emerged with her new hat and handbag and got into the Jeep. The kids, not wanting to miss a trip to town, jumped in also. It was a vicarious thing, at best. Ten-year-old Will Jr. told his mother what to do. Left foot pedal down, push starter button, etc. After all, Willie had been watching Pa do it for years and he drove the Ford 9N tractor so his father, standing on the hay wagon could shoot night rabbits (meat on the table). They lurched forward, stalled it, tried again and they were off. Steering was somewhat different from the reins of the pony. They went down in a ditch and back up on the road and down in the ditch on the other side with the kids squealing with delight and hanging on for dear life. By the time they got to the main road Daisy got so she didn't over compensate, and they headed for town with Willie shifting gears and giving instructions.

Daisy did all her shopping, loaded the stuff in the Jeep and felt pretty proud of herself (a liberated woman for the first time in her entire life), so she treated all the kids to ice cream cones.

(This true story was related to me by Bernadine Kruse.)

45

Driving Mrs. Daisy, Part 2

Being able to drive was one of the nicest things that ever happened to Daisy. Of course, she still had to use the outhouse and pump water by hand with a pitcher pump. But now she could run errands for Will, visit with neighbors and occasionally, when Will was around the buildings to watch the kids, she could sneak off with the Jeep and explore back roads and fire trails and enjoy the lovely Montana scenery. Such moments gave her a serenity she had never before known.

Then one day, Will's brother called long distance from Missouri to tell Will that the manager on the spread where he worked had quit. The rich owners had made his brother boss. They needed another man and Will could have the job. The pay was good. The house had heat, a bathroom and a garden plot. There would be a side of beef every year. This required a lot of discussion and pillow talk, but it was decided that they could better themselves by making the move. It was a tough decision to leave what they called home, but they called the auctioneer and proceeded to sort through a lifetime's accumulation and get almost everything in the barn ready for the sale. After the auctioneer banged the gavel for the last time, they had more money than they ever had before but sad, sad memories.

The next day they loaded up for their move. Daisy had insisted they keep Grandma's good china. She also took her canned tomatoes and canned beef.[1,2] After all, they had to eat when they got there. She did, however, give her jellies and preserves to the neighbor ladies whom she knew could use them.

Will had insisted that they take along his saddle horse. He was a man of his time and had never been without a horse. After all, he'd need a horse on the new job and they might not have one for him. So, he put the horse in his horse trailer hooked behind his '41 Chevy ¾ ton pickup, which was loaded down with furniture and covered with a canvas. The kids decided who they were going to ride with. Daisy took the '47 Ford sedan, which was packed full of boxes and just like the "Oakies" 20 years earlier, they set off to find a better life.

Will led the way with the pickup, as it was slower and loaded heavy and Daisy tried to keep him in sight. They had mapped out the route but the trip was not uneventful. They got lost a few times, got separated a few times, got angry a few times and had a few flat tires. It was a memorable trip through South Dakota, Nebraska and Kansas and then it happened...

In some city with a square (not unlike Easton or Gettysburg), where the major state roads converge, Daisy stalled the Ford. She pumped the accelerator a half-dozen times and pushed the starter button again. She pumped the accelerator some more as she had seen Will do and then she choked it. (You never choke a flathead Ford if it has been run that day.)

(Continued on next page)

Driving Mrs. Daisy, Part 2 (*continued*)

A trolley car clanged its bell and couldn't make its swing. Big trucks, with 35-foot Fruehoff trailers, blew their horns, GMC dump trucks with 671 Detroit Diesels made evil noises...and there was Daisy, in a cold sweat, as a big policeman came up and said, "All right lady, get out of the car." The kids piled out also and stood terrified on the sidewalk. The officer got the Ford started and pulled it into an empty parking spot and told Daisy that they could go.

They arrived at the new place, unloaded a few blankets and some canned goods, and all fell asleep exhausted. The very next day, Daisy, before she unpacked, went to the county seat and got her learner's permit for her first driver's license.

(True story as related to me by Bernadine Kruse)

1 Canned beef, canned with the hot pack method, is really good!

2 As a wedding gift, my son received a quart mason jar full of canned beef: it was labeled "First Husband."

Smarty Pants

Horace's father had a Fordson Tractor and a Messinger (made in nearby Tatamy, PA) threshing machine, with which they did custom work throughout the county. Horace's job, among other things, was to work the throttle lever as the sheaves of grain were pitched onto the feed table, since the Fordsons were all built without a governor. Twelve-year-old Horace also drove the tractor and 'thrasher' between farms with his father following him in an old 1921 Model T Ford service truck. Fordsons had steel wheels with angle iron cleats and rode hard.

This particular day, Father took the tractor and left Horace to drive the truck to the next job site. He was pleased and, oh, so, proud, in spite of having no shoes and only threadbare Oshkosh overalls. Soon he would be driving through town and everybody would see him and see how grown up he was. But, after a while, the Model T steered hard, and Horace got out to find that the right front tire was low...out came the bicycle pump and Horace struggled to pump it back up. He was then able to go in high gear to catch up. Oh, the thrill of such speed and of not having to constantly hold the low gear pedal to the floor.

By the time he caught up to the Fordson, he had another steering problem and he had to pump up the tire again. Soon he figured out why his father had let him drive the truck. The tire had a slow leak and about once a mile, it needed more air. Sure enough, it was down again right in the middle of town where he had hoped to impress the locals (especially the girls) with his driving ability.

But he would make up for it all. He would show the townies how strong he was and how fast he could pump up a 30x3½ tire. So he started pumping as fast and as hard as he could, really leaning on the pump handle with all the power of his skinny muscles. Up and down and up and down he went and then the pain and realization of what was happening. He had forgotten about the crotch being out of his overalls. The old guys sitting on the courthouse steps had one of the best laughs of their lives and Horace was a sadder but wiser lad for it all.

* * * * * * *

Grandpa was a farmer,

Alone he worked by hand,

He chewed and spat Red Man,

With horses he farmed our land.

His son just loved the Fordson,

A love Gramps never felt,

He hated that gray Fordson,

Just like he hated Roosevelt.

All Creatures Great and Shep

A lot of things have changed since James Herriot practiced veterinary medicine: sulfa drugs, penicillin vaccines, x-rays and surgical procedures that were only hoped for sixty years ago are now routine. And a lot of things are still the same, with concerned animal owners calling in the middle of the night, dogs and cats getting hit by cars, horses getting cut and cows still having twins all tangled up inside and occasionally expelling the uterus along with the calf. This latter usually occurs in some God-forsaken mud hole and takes herculean efforts to correct.

Old Doc Sliker made farm calls years ago. The farmers were always glad to see him come for emergencies because the loss of a single horse or cow was a catastrophe to a subsistence farm during the Great Depression. The kids liked to see Doc come, as he always had a candy for each one, and if you were lucky, he'd give you the little glass toy car in which the candies came. All dogs received a biscuit too- as he got out of his car.

Doc kept all of his medicines, tools and equipment in the trunk of his car. He bought a new car every two years and never bothered to change the oil or wash it. He would have it greased when he bought new tires, every ten to twenty thousand miles, as cord tires did not last long on high crowned dirt roads. He preferred coupes with large trunks. My Grandpap had a police dog Old Shep could do no wrong in Grandpap's eyes. He kept groundhogs under control, stray cats and salesmen away. Shep did love to chase cars and occasionally caught one and would come back all mangled up. Doc Sliker patched him up a couple of times. Shep liked Doc, or at least the dog biscuits Doc brought along. Shep always made a big friendly fuss when the veterinarian came.

Doc had been driving a Reo Flying Cloud coupe and he traded it in on a new 1937 Packard coupe. When Doc arrived at our place, Shep ran out to meet him, accepted the dog biscuit and then proceeded to inspect and squirt on all four wheels. This kid thought that Packard was just about the nicest car I'd ever seen (I still do). I also thought that the dog had awfully poor manners.

Doc got out of the car, put a big chew of Redman in his mouth, got his medicine bag out of the trunk and put on his galoshes. Doc went into the barn followed by Shep and as he was taking the sick cow's temperature with a rectal thermometer, Shep sneaked up behind Doc and took a nip of his leg just above his boot. Doc instantaneously spit out his chewing tobacco - juice and all - and it hit Shep right between the eyes. Shep let out a "Yipp" and headed for the far end of the barn, skidding his head and eyes up against the hay bales as he went. Shep then laid himself down with his nose on his paws and glowered at the veterinarian. After that, every time Doc came, he would put his tail between his legs and run for the far end of the barn and sulk.

(Continued on next page)

All Creatures Great and Shep *(continued)*

This went on for two years, until Doc traded his Packard in on a brand new 1939 Chrysler coupe with a trunk which was bigger than the body of our 1934 Chevy half ton pickup. Doc went into the barn and was listening to a cow's chest with a stethoscope, when he realized that Shep was lying upside down on Doc's feet with his paws up and was whimpering. Doc reached down and petted Shep who jumped up and stood close by just wagging his tail as hard as he could.

Modern science has not figured out what goes through a dog's mind but it seems as though old Shep simply didn't like Packard's or Redman tobacco juice. Maybe it was a Packard that ran over his snout.

It Ain't Necessarily So

Those of us with antique cars kind of take it for granted that the public enjoys seeing our self-propelled antiques. This isn't always the case, as was evidenced on our June 1st tour, when as our tour leader, I pulled into the wrong driveway. The owner of that property was absolutely incensed at our trespassing and presence.

It was an embarrassing situation for all concerned – particularly for our hosts who had opened their home to show us their collection of antiques, antique cars, seashells, quilts and original paintings.

We must bear in mind that some people consider us just another nuisance to be dealt with and we must be ever mindful of our manners when dealing with others.

My apologies to those who were on the club's Antiquities Tour for those difficult moments. Hopefully, we can look back at that incident and someday laugh about it.

Antique Car tour stopping on Interstate 78 bridge over the Delaware River before the highway was open to the public.

The Last Farmer's Last Wish

I went to the field the other day,
All alone to bale the hay,
A red-tailed hawk caught a snake,
Soon from him the crows do take.

All around the swallows swoop,
Opened mouthed, bugs they scoop,
Vesper sparrows and Bobolinks,
Like it here- so me thinks.

On wintertime the Arctic Owl,
Over my fields he loves to prowl,
Harriers hover over the hill,
Waiting, looking to make a kill.

That big old oak that once stood tall,
To the ground at last did fall.
Who will care for this land,
When like the oak I cannot stand?

Ike, Arthur and Harry Frey,
Better men by far than I,
All worked this land all their lives,
And loved it like they loved their wives.

My sons left for other things,
And love not the smells of springs,
Above the fields that alone I culture,
Surveys all a turkey vulture.

If to heaven I'm not a guest,
Lord, grant me one request,
Like that buzzard may I soar over all,
And not worry about cholesterol.

Saturday Night Dead

There is a lot of violence in our society today and there is a lot of violence on television. Any connection? But it didn't used to be that way. Sixty years ago about the only violence young folks were exposed to was an occasional fist fight at school or in going to the movies. Sometimes going to the movies was an adventure in itself.

Furman saved his money and when he was old enough to drive, he had $35 saved up for a well-used Model A Ford Tudor. He had mowed lawns, pulled mustard, stacked hay and shoveled snow. His kid brothers, Ephram and Myron, were doing likewise and expected to go along to the Saturday night movies.

The Fords had to be parked on a hill so that it would kick start. Early Model A's had an alternator and would stay running with a dead battery, which this Model A always had.

The first stop was to buy gas at "Slow Joe's" gas station, and then they headed for town. They parked at the top of Neuman's Hill with the front wheel cut toward the curb, transmission in low gear, emergency brake set tight and with Myron putting a wedge of firewood ahead of a rear wheel. Then they walked the six blocks to the 'El Rancho' theater making sure they got there in time to see the very end of the previous show plus the 'Funny Pitchurs'. They then relaxed to enjoy the (good guys versus bad guys) Grade B western which was the high spot of their week – or so they thought.

This particular fall evening after they had their Pepsi Cola ("twice as much for a nickel too, Pepsi Cola is the drink for you"), they hiked back up the hill to get the car. Furman turned on the switch and twisted the steering wheel as 'Eph' kicked the front tire away from the curb and Myron retrieved his wheel chock. They scrambled on to the running board and into the car as the Model A coasted down the hill and coughed to life. The brakes were pretty good for slowing down although not much good for stopping. But they safely made it through the intersection and onto South Main Street and out of town on the Brunswick Pike.

Constable Pyatt noticed they had no headlights and decided to follow. 'Eph' saw the police car and told Furnan to turn into Apgar's corn field. Across the bumpy corn stubble they went until the Model A stopped dead behind a big corn shock. The battery had fallen out! They piled out and ran the last two miles home as fast as they could, laughing all the way.

'Twas the Night
(with apologies to Clement Moore)

'Twas' the month before Christmas and all thru the region,[1]

No car shows were held, not even a smidgen,

With antiques hacked up in garages with care,

In the hopes that the rust wouldn't get in there,

With me in my long johns and wife in her quilt,

After going to church to assuage all our guilt

When what to our wondering ears should we hear,

But a big block V-8, floored, in second gear.

Throughout all the hills the echo did ring,

My thoughts, of course, went to antiques and to Spring,

Memories of car shows danced all through my head,

Until my wife, in anguish, she said:

"Wake up, my dear spouse: he's right on our lawn!!"

And right at this point, my awareness did dawn.

I grabbed up my shotgun and turned on the light,

And there midst the holly was a horrible sight.

Doing donuts galore in the mud and the muck,

Was a high-rider pickup that was almost stuck.

As all four fat tires continued to spin,

For our guest had found a 20th century sin.

He'd seen it on TV and it looked like such fun,

But then the driver spotted me and my gun.

So putting his thumb right up to his nose,

He wiggled his fingers and then off he goes.

If I had shot him, I'd been put in jail,

Mid hopes that this region would post me my bail.

So happy motoring to all, for it is such fun,

And remember my friends—hide those shells for your gun!

---

[1] Region in this book refers to the Lehigh Region of the Antique Automobile Club of America, for which I have been writing these bits of odd knowledge for 25 years.

730 Rock

Of those of us who till these lands,
Few are into heavy metal bands.
Farmers, by and large, are pretty straight,
To us Led Zeppelin ain't too great.
That music doesn't turn us on,
We opt for tunes of days bygone.
But long-haired types with purple sneakers,
Use moving vans to haul in speakers.
Their sound cranked up to eighty amps,
Can even be heard by our Gramps.
They bounce and yell and holler loud,
To entertain a spaced-out crowd,
And bang and toot into their mikes,
Their vested fans on Harley bikes.
Soak up all those throbbing vibes,
Like souped up old primeval tribes.
Farmers think that they are nuts,
With sound felt down into their guts.
How can they stand all that noise,
That makes deaf men out of boys?
But those of us who've been around,
Know truly heavy metal sound,
Comes from inside old John Deeres.
For stack music I give my cheers.
The diesel ones built round nineteen fifty,
Will give a buzz that's mighty nifty.
I'll give you kids with orange hair,
A free concert that's pretty fair.
Have your own Woodstock recital,
Let her run at a good fast idle.
Put your tender low-fi ears,
Down upon the camshaft gears.
And I'll hold your gourd hard on the block,
Like, man, that's heavy metal rock!

STUPID NEWLEYWEDS

<u>Story #1</u>: Trudy and I got married in 1951 (I'm pretty sure), and we purchased a brick home at 100 Snyders Road and fixed it up. My wife *Insisted* that she could not have the outhouse behind the house. It simply did not look good. I thought the outhouse was alright as outhouses went: it was a good place to keep the lawnmower, the rakes and the shovels and stuff for the garden. But, IT HAD TO GO.

And it just so happened that a neighbor down the road named Leslie Rowe lived in an old stone house and had a bunch of kids, and quite a number of old cars, and they needed a new outhouse.

Bingo! Solution.

So, we loaded our outhouse on a hay wagon and took it down, and the Rowes had dug a new hole to set their new outhouse on. We unloaded it somehow – I don't recall how we did it... we did it with manpower, I guess.

Meanwhile, back up at the brick house which was an American Four-Square that my grandfather built in 1914 (I firmly believe that it was a Sears Kit Home and they got it pre-assembled or precut with railroad siding and hauled it home). My grandfather, a hired man, my father who was a teenager at the time, and a carpenter put the house up. But we *"couldn't* have the outhouse by it."

So here we had an empty hole where the outhouse had been, and I got dirt, filled that in, leveled it all off, stomped it down, and planted grass. Two problems were solved...or so we thought.

Come the following Spring, the ground was frozen on top and we had a hard rain: then we had water in the cellar. Not only was it water, but it was sewage water. Here the water had gone down into the outhouse pit as the ground thawed out and we had one real mess. It taught us a lot. We did know water rain downhill, but we found out that other stuff ran downhill, too.

STUPID NEWLEYWEDS (continued)

Story #2: The brick house had a cistern and relied on rainwater from the roof into the rainspouts and it emptied out into the cistern. My grandparents had used this as a source of water in the house for years. Nobody got sick that I know of, but obviously it wasn't the cleanest. What usually happened that it would start to rain, and you wait maybe five minutes before you emptied the water into the cistern because the rain would wash of the slate dust and the bird poop and so you let that run on the ground before you would divert water into the cistern.

So before my wife and I could move in, we decided to clean out that cistern which hadn't been used for a couple years. I went down to the barn and got myself some dairy chlorine, and I went down into the cistern and scrubbed down the walls with water and had a shovel to clean up the stuff as best I could. And then I decided to sanitize that thing so I threw chlorine around – I threw A LOT of chlorine around: and then it dawned on me that that stuff was bad stuff and I better get out of there real quick. I had a homemade ladder in the cistern, and I just barely made it out.

* * * * * * *

PRESBYTERIAN GOTHIC

Pastor Rebecca Seegar with Bob Frey at Old Greenwich Presbyterian 2016's "Wear your work clothes to church" Sunday. Note Bob holding his hat in lieu of a pitchfork.   (*Photo courtesy of Kathy Ahart*)

I Wipe the Pipe

I wipe the pipe, I pump the gas
I rub the hub and scrub the glass
I check the clutch, I mop the top
I poke the choke, I sell the pop
I clear the gear, I block the knock
I jack the back, I set the clock
So join the ranks of those who know
And fill your tank with Texaco. *

*There is still a Sunoco station which will do all that for free plus check your oil and tire pressure. It is at Hemmings, in Bennington, Vermont

From Uncle Milton Berle's Texaco Star theater

Stecker's Esso served all those functions but in addition was the unofficial community center on Saturday nights. That's when OLD timers with nothing better to do, as well as kids with only bikes to drive, would gather. Older kids with jalopies and some gas in the tank, would cruise around some and then drop by also. During hot summer months Dorney Park offered stock car racing. Modified 37 Ford coupes mostly but occasionally 49 Plymouths and Oldsmobiles would battle it out on Dorney Parks quarter-mile track. But all year round, it was almost as much fun to sit on soda crates around Mr. Stecker's Esso and watch the action that was absolutely FREE!

Everybody went out Saturday night, to drive in movies, hot dog stands, saloons or night clubs, for a myriad of reasons and most of them went around Stecker's circle at some point.

Some obscure highway engineer figured that the secret to efficient traffic flow was tight traffic circles with cars coming in and out tangently. Brits call them roundabouts.

Drivers on Route 22 who hadn't seen a traffic light since Harrisburg or Somerville would come to this circle entirely too fast, with their bias ply balloon tires squealing. Once somebody went right through Stecker's Esso gas pumps and everybody scattered.

Clean Green Limericks

A farmer from Amity Hall,
Loved his red International Farmall,
Until helping one year,
He drove a neighbor's John Deere,
Now he won't use his Farmall at all.

An old man from out near Boise,
Collects green Ertl toysies,
But now his dear wife,
Once the joy of his life,
Claims he creeps around making 'putt-putt noises.

There was a man from Monroe,
To all the sales he did go,
But who would have thunk,
He's got so much junk,
That his lawn is an old tractor show.

There is an oldster named Ribicoff,
At whom neighbors all did scoff,
He worked hard every year,
With a two-cylinder Deere,
But his farm mortgage now is all paid off.

There once was a collector named Jacques,
Who slammed on his pickup truck brakes.
When he saw 9x36 tires,
In the bushes and briars,
And stepped on a nest full of snakes.

An elegant lady from Lyle,
Whose husband worked all the while,
Up to his elbows in grease,
Restoring each tractor piece,
So she shot him Godfather style.

There was a man from Toledo
While fixing his Wico Magneto
Held onto the cap,
Gave the impulse a snap,
And dropped it right on his feet...OH! *

There was an old farmer from here,
Who restored and adored a John Deere,
So his wife got a divorce,
Got the farm too, of course,
So his is a very dear Deere.

There is an editor from Bee,
Whose magazines we can't wait to see,
For he edits this stuff,
Some of it pretty rough,
Like poems and limericks by me.

*My dad Harry H. Frey actually did this & dropped the magneto on Mom's new linoleum.

"Link and Ruth"

Link and Ruth's kids lived next door to and played around the family's sawmill...not the safest place in the world, but 'Link' kept one eye on them and they never got hurt. They saved their father a lot of steps by bringing him tools and putting them away. (Today DYFUS, Division of Youth and Family Services, would probably put the kids in a foster home and the parents in jail.

The sawmill had originally been powered by a water wheel but had been converted at some point with a huge old General Electric motor (the size of a beer keg) with open brushes sparkling away and emitting ozone (not too safe either). This ran the flat belt system with overhead shafting that had pillow blocks and pulleys, and it drove the machinery that made peach baskets.

The boys went to the woods when the workmen cut timber and they played in the woods. As they got older, they used their hatchets to lop off small upper limbs and later graduated to using axes.

When Ken got old enough to reach the pedals of the International T-20 crawler tractor, it was his job to snake the logs down to where they could be loaded onto the log truck. Child labor-laws do not apply to family labor, but there is currently legislation at federal level to do so.

Ken's favorite lunch in the woods was a sandwich warmed up on the valve cover and a can of Campbell's soup dropped down the exhaust pipe of the idling T-20. When hot, he would open the throttle and the can would fly out like a mortar.

The family also owned timber in Canada and once they got over the border, Link would let 13-year-old Ken drive the trailer truck and the father would take a nice nap.

A few years later, (during WW II) they needed lumber from Canada and since help was unavailable, Link decided to send Ken. Mrs. Rapp was adamant: "You can't send a fifteen-year-old boy all the way up there alone, I won't allow it!"

"Oh, he knows the way up there well enough, and he is really good at handling the cab-over-engine International with trailer behind. He can double-clutch, shift the two-speed axle and back up as well as I can," was Link's reply. Mother asked, "What if something should happen?" Eventually, the mother gave in but insisted somebody else absolutely had to go along with Ken. "OK," was Link's reply. "We will send Bobby along." And so, a fifteen-year-old and his twelve-year-old brother set out with the 1940 cab-over-engine International on the first of many 'international' trips.

Volunteer!

My son, Rob, and I attended the Model T Ford Club of America's 100th Celebration of the first Model T car that was held July 2003 in Richmond, Indiana. No, we did not take as planned our 1917 Touring car but after a total elapsed travel time of thirteen hours (including four and half hours sitting in a 737 on the tarmac in Philadelphia Airport), we figured out that we could and should have trailered the Model T Ford the 675 miles. There were over 900 other Model T cars there and no two were exactly alike since the owners had made modifications in one way or other in last 80 years. Also present were Model A and Model B Fords, V8-Fords, stock cars, dragsters, hot rods and custom cars by the thousands.

In 2003, when Ford motor company had its 100th Anniversary somebody in the Club of America got the brainstorm to have a birthday party honoring the car that put America on wheels. They pulled it off with all volunteer help. Admittedly, Richmond, Indiana, is not the 'Big Apple' and there might not be too much going on there in the middle of corn and soybean fields. With the help of the city and the county fairgrounds, it was a complete success thanks to the volunteers. And volunteerism is what makes our own little club and this country great. Thanks again, everybody.

Styling Changes

From the mid-1920s through the 1980s, there were styling changes in cars every year. During the 30s into the 50s, Harley Earl was in charge of styling at General Motors. Dick Gregory designed for Ford. There were independents like Ray Dietrich and Dutch Darrin who worked with Pierce Arrow and Packard. In addition, there were independent industrial designers, Raymond Lowey and Dreyfus Engineering, (who designed for Studebaker.) His theme was, "form follows with function," whatever that means.

In the late 1930s, all the farm machinery manufacturers decided that they should also style and 'streamline' their tractors, even though wind resistance is not much of a problem at seven miles per hour. John Deere hired the famous Raymond Lowey. He came up with a neo-art deco grill with horizontal bars and a hood with a foot-wide ridge that started over the narrow front wheels and continued back to the dash which was just under the steering wheel. The air intake and the exhaust protruded up through the center of the hood.

Fast forward to 1950. The muffler went out on Roy's 1940 Model A John Deere. Not only did it make an ear-splitting pop, pop, pop noise when the tractor was under load but it blew stinking exhaust fumes right back in his face. Roy always tried to take care of his stuff and every winter, he curry-combed his cows and Simonized the hood and fenders of his John Deere. He had heard that the easy way to replace the muffler on a John Deere was to take a hammer and cold chisel and cut a six-inch square hole in the hood to access the four bolts that held the muffler. He first looked under the hood with a flashlight and decided it was just too much of a job for him to tackle himself. He figured out that it was necessary to take six bolts out of the radiator shell, another six out of the dash, unbolt the cap off of the steering gear box, sop up the grease, screw the steering worm out of the gear box, drain the gas tank and lift off the hood and gas tank. He was proud of his tractor and didn't want to damage the hood, so he called the local John Deere dealer to send out their mechanic.

It so happened that the day the George V. Seiple and Son mechanic arrived to install the muffler, Roy was away from the farm all day. When he looked at his tractor, he found that Seiple's mechanic had used a hammer and chisel on the hood. Roy was absolutely furious, called up Mr. Seiple, gave him a "piece of his mind" and swore that he would never, ever buy anything from Seiple again. So much for Raymond Lowey's Form Follows with Function Design. (See page 183)

If You Live Long Enough

In 1941, Chevrolet upstaged Ford by enclosing the running boards with flared doors, and now running boards are back on ritzy upscale sport utility vehicles like the big Lincoln Navigator.[1] People who would never drive a truck in the past are driving 'trucks' in the form of big SUVs, which the manufacturers are happy to sell, because of high profit margins due to the parts interchangeability between SUVs and half-ton pickups. People who cannot remember the big cars of the 1930's are choosing big, high, roomy vehicles with chair height seating and a frame underneath. Is there some kind of extra sensory memory lurking in the minds of today's yuppies? Or do they feel safer in a heavy and formidable vehicle? Or is it some kind of denial of federal emission standards since SUVs conform to the less strict 'truck' standards?

Years ago, all kinds of things were hauled on running boards and held on with clothesline or baling wire. Telescoping, pantograph type things, were available to clamp onto the running boards to enable people to haul stuff they didn't want in the car itself.

Years ago, my father-in-law and his cronies went deep sea fishing at Toms River, caught a bunch of blues and headed home with the catch iced in a bucket that was tied to the side of his Oldsmobile. The highway department had a bumpy detour on the Black Horse Pike and when they got home, all the fish had bounced and sloshed out. The womenfolk didn't believe their fish story at all.

I wonder if and when some Madison Avenue type will rediscover my Motometer as they did running boards and the four on the floor shift.

[1] A person could not get into them if Navigators did not have steps.

Reading, Writing and Arithmetic

I am the product of a one-room school, in case you hadn't figured it out: 32 kids, eight grades and one teacher. Reading, writing and arithmetic studies were grouped with two grades taught together. Kindergarten and first, etc. Everybody was exposed to history and geography and absorbed what they could. During study hour, the older kids helped the younger ones with their homework. During recess, the kids were turned loose and left to their own devices (baseball, football and 'Ant Tony over the schoolhouse roof) with the teacher banging on the window when things got rowdy. The teacher got to know each kid individually. The kids knew their teacher and their identity within the group. The pecking order got shook out pretty quickly. This in contrast to modern, consolidated, regionalized schools where teachers don't know the students and when somebody "disses" somebody, a shooting may occur. But all good things must come to an end. There were two outhouses out back and the drinking water came from a cistern (underground storage facility) which was replenished by runoff from the school's slate roof. Some slats fell off the belfry and the pigeons moved in and did their dirty business on the schoolhouse roof.

It was decided in midyear that the water wasn't safe to drink, so every day two boys were sent with a Gott galvanized water cooler to haul water from the spring a couple of hundred yards away. The only problem being that the spring was located in Mr. Snyder's cow pasture and cows being cows it became necessary to close the school at the end of the school year.

So, the following year we went to the 'BIG' school, which had two rooms, lower grades in one room, with fifth, sixth and seventh in the other room. The boys at this school had the reputation for being bad. During recess, they once pushed Mr. Beer's hay rake into the creek and his plow in a culvert. They also stole eggs from a neighbor lady's henhouse, lightly cracked them and put them in the rafters of the girl's outhouse.

When I was in fifth grade, 'Big Bob' was in sixth—when I was in sixth, he was in sixth and when I was in seventh he was in sixth. He was not a very good student but school was preferable to working in his grandfather's barn and there were lots of opportunities in school for practical jokes. His best buddy was "Little Floyd", who could dream up lots of interesting capers. The teacher, Mrs. D., did her very best to cope with them and to keep some semblance of order. It was a long school year for her. On the very last day of school, the boys loosened the Schrader tire stem valves on the passenger side of her 1937 Packard and she ruined two irreplaceable tires in the midst of World War II. That was the last we ever saw of Mrs. D.

The following year we had a new teacher, Miss G. who arrived in a 1934 Ford V8 convertible. We were impressed. She was reputed to be a 'Fizz Ed' major-whatever that was—and was fully as big as 'Big Bob' - maybe bigger.

We found out what Fizz-ed was when Floyd swore. Miss George picked him up and washed his mouth out with yellow liquid soap.

The Great Cattle Drive

There never was a problem with the old covered bridge, since it looked and smelled just like a barn with an opening at the other end. The new bridge, built in 1904, was another story, with its wire rope suspension system, which looked flimsy to both man and beast. Most horses would cross it with some persuasion but of course horses had blinders. Blinders were six-inch squares made of leather and sewn into their halters, which prevented horses from being frightened by things off to the side. Cows didn't wear blinders and were easily spooked by all kinds of things. As far as anyone knew, nobody had driven a cow herd across in the eleven years since the new bridge had been linking the two Riegelsvilles, but it just had to be done.

April 1st was 'moving' day every year as tenants and landlords both tried to better themselves as leases ran out. The better farmers tended to gravitate to the farms owned by the wealthy families, such as the Clines, Miexels and Riegels. These farmers did their very best to be good tenants. While today it might be seen as paternalistic, it was not a bad system.

Although the arrangements varied, the landlord usually provided the land, the house and barns and half of the inputs, such as seed and lime. He also got one-half of the crop and paid the taxes. The tenant provided the other half of the inputs, all the equipment, all the labor and was allowed to keep a limited number of livestock, as long as he spread all of the manure back on the land. Thus, a tenant with limited assets, good luck, good weather, good neighbors and lots of hard work, could make a living, feed his family well, and maybe even buy his own farm.

Although it was an outgrowth of the Feudal System, the share crop arrangement worked well for centuries, as long as everyone was honest. Therein was the inherent problem and the result was a substantial reshuffling every spring as tenants moved.

'Uncle' Dan King had heard that the Riegel farm would be vacant in 1915 and approached the Riegel family,[1] since he had a good reputation, a lease was signed. The only problem was that the farm was in Pennsylvania and 'Uncle' farmed at Creek Road and Mountain Road in Pohatcong Township, NJ.

On the appointed day, they moved the household goods first thing in the morning. Then they returned for the animals, closing the bars to the various fields en route. Bars were cedar saplings stripped of their limbs and placed across gateways to fields. Most fields had stone rows or 'barb' wire fences but there were orchards and unfenced areas that had to be guarded.

More neighbors had arrived with their boys, who were excused from school. George Snyder brought Harold and Donald. Art Frey brought his twelve-year old son Harry. Harry H. Frey was my father and Arthur J. Frey my grandfather. Although he was well into his seventies, my great

(Continued on next page)

65

The Great Cattle Drive *(continued)*

'Grandpap Ike' Frey was along with his horse and buggy,[2] mostly because he didn't want to miss out on the fun (chasing cows is fun if they are somebody else's cows), The Fair, Scott, Hager, King and Mellick families were all well represented, too.

'Uncle Dan' led the way with some sweet-smelling timothy hay on his wagon calling, "Kooh bos, sookie, sookie, sookie." Young men and boys ran alongside of the cattle on the edge of the dirt road. It was imperative to keep the cows on Mountain Road and not allow any of them to go down Cemetery Road. The intersection of Mountain Road and Pinchers Point Road was scary (as it is today) but they managed to turn the animals and safely get them down the steep part and past the old Seyler Barn on River Road, where they turned the animals south on River Road. Everybody hoped no trains would spook the cows since the Bel-Del Railroad was close to the road.

When they got to the Roebling Bridge, the problems really started. The cows refused to cross and milled around. Patrons piled out of the three-story hotel with the mansard roof, hooting and hollering. The animals would not step off of the dirt road onto the bridge's planking. Shoving, whipping, tail twisting and cursing simply did not work. (Don't tell PETA.) Then, on a whim, one of the Scott boys pursed his lips and made a buzzing sound while humming to emulate the sound bot flies[3] make before they sting cattle. A heifer raised her tail and charged across the bridge with the bull right behind her and the rest of the beasts (a dozen) followed. 'Uncle' Dan had to whip up his team to get out of the way. They had done what folks thought could not be done: they had driven a cow herd over the Roebling suspension bridge.

[1] The Riegel family owned three p'aper mills in the Delaware River Valley.

[2] Still in our Wagon House

[3] Bot flies sting cattle on their rumps, and the maggots migrate to the animals' backs at which time they are known as warbles and become pea pod-sized zits.

Hometown

Carpentersville was a busy little town in the nineteenth century, especially after the Belvidere and Delaware Railroad (1) was completed in 1853. It was founded by the Carpenter family in the late seventeenth century and had previously been a Leni-Lenape settlement (2). It was an ideal spot for a settlement with an ever-flowing spring, a nearby river (3) (with lots of fish) which made travel easy, and the site was a bit warmer and less windy than the surrounding Pohatcong (4) hills.

Carpentersville extends about a mile, and the center of the white man's settlement was the country store with its supply of rubber boots, denim overalls, bolts of cloth, notions, Porter's Lineament and Salve, harness repairs, cracker and pickle barrels, canned goods, salted cod, fresh fish, clams and oysters (5) on ice. Fresh warm bread and rolls arrived on the 7 AM train from Phillipsburg.

Rear view of the building once the Carpentersville country store. The bottom left window still has the original iron security bars.

It only took three hours to travel from the Jersey shore to the Carpentersville store in the late 1800's. Supplies (dynamite and rock

(Continued on next page)

Hometown *(continued)*

drills) for the various quarries arrived by rail. My great-grandmother shopped at Wanamaker's in Philadelphia (6) which was only one hour away by train.

Carpentersville was a self-sufficient town until the advent of the motor car, gradually putting the store out of business when the Pennsylvania Railroad stopped hauling mail in 1951. The store building was purchased and remodeled by Donald Snyder, and the first tenants were the Schneck family some 70 years ago.

Front view of old store in 2017

(1) Known as the "Bel-Del."
(2) Several archeological digs (one going on at this writing in 2017) and lots of arrowheads and flint chips have been found.
(3) Delaware
(4) "Pohatcong" was the Indian name for "between the hills."
(5) Oyster pie.
(6) See "Ike and Charlotte" in my previous book <u>Behind the Motormeter</u>.
(7) There were at least twenty lime kilns from Carpentersville to Phillipsburg. Limestone was quarried for the many nearby dwellings and burned in kilns to make mortar for cement.

Carpentersville Station circa 1930s looking north.

Mother's Day Thoughts

It occurs to me that there are a lot of long suffering women associated with the antique car hobby. Mothers or not, they are mothers of over-grown little boys and their over-grown toys. They are amazed that their men can find a goofenator pump for a 1931 basket case (out in 200 acres of Hershey mud) but can't find their own socks!

To them I dedicate this poem:

An elegant lady from Lyle,
Whose husband spent all of his while,
Up to his elbows in grease,
Restoring every last piece,
So she shot him, godfather style.

The view from behind the muffler.

We all lived in a Yellow Studebaker

As far as I know, we were the only generation that ever played hooky from Sunday School or church service. We were from good Christian families with good parents trying to bring us up "right". In fact, Dick's mother taught our Sunday School class and my mother taught the teenage girl's Sunday School. Our hooky evolved over the years from running on the cemetery's stone wall, playing King of the Mountain on said wall, or hide and seek in the cemetery. Our parents had to know this because of torn pants and scuffed-up Sunday shoes. It was perhaps a form of rebellion against parental authority and religious indoctrination.

As we got old enough to drive, we would occasionally skip church, if somebody had their old jalopy. In fact, I once almost upset 'Brud's' brand-new Pontiac taking a right angle turn entirely too fast.

Dick's father had recently gotten a brand new, shiny, yellow 1950 Studebaker four-door with a big V-8. We all piled in one nice spring Sunday. There were Dick, Jeff, 'Brud', Donald, Roy and two Billy's an me; so the car was pretty well loaded down. There was no Interstate system yet, so we could not see how fast the car would go. The rural roads were narrow, high-crowned macadam. We tore down Still Valley Road, through the Jersey Central Railroad tunnel, past Cole's Mill and – whoops—there was another car on the one-lane creek bridge. Brakes squealed as we went down over the creek bank, stopping just short of disaster!

I won't say we got religion at this point, but that sure cured us of skipping church.

Be Prepared

People carry amazing things around with them. Women's handbags contain all kinds of junk.

Not to be outdone, men also carry around a lot of stuff. Office people have pens and pencils, engineers once used slide rules but now have hand-held devices and tradesmen can carry a whole tool chest in belted-on saddlebags. Today, those in the public eye carry combs, nail files and even some masculine makeup items. Chain drive key rings can be found on maintenance men and truck drivers. Farmers usually carry Swiss army knives, but I, personally, carry a six-inch Vise Grip on the premise that vise grips will cut string but a knife won't cut wire or unscrew a nut. Once I even knew a guy who carried a magnifying glass. His name was Vic Banas (a departed member of our club). He and his wife were one of those delightful couples, (I've written about them before) whom I would never have met, had it not been for this antique car hobby.

Several years ago at a Lehigh Valley Region banquet, we had a belly dancer as entertainment. Since there was no stage at that fire hall, our dancer performed on the dance floor between the head table and the guest. Therefore, we had to crane our necks to see.

Toward the end of her performance the young lady trotted down the aisles, doing her stuff in time to the oriental music. When she got to Vic Banas, he whipped out his trusty magnifying glass and carefully examined her NAVEL.

Moral of the story- Be prepared for anything in this New Year. Happy New Year!!

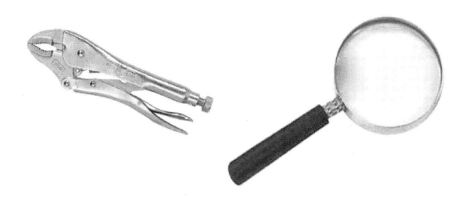

"Always the Dullness of the Fool
is the Whetstone of the Wits"

Shakespeare – *As You Like It*

Raymond had this terrible addiction. It got worse every year and was really bad in the hot summer weather. He was an only child. His father was dead and his mother raised him all by herself. He was just a bit odd and was tall and thin with great big ears, slightly hard of hearing and had a bit of a speech impediment so that he 'tawkled a widdle pit twooked.'

Kids can be cruel and starting back in kindergarten, they teased Raymond unmercifully so that his mother eventually tutored him at home. Thus, he grew up isolated from other children and never developed certain necessary social skills. A troubled youth lacking self-esteem before anybody had heard of those terms. He was devoted and caring and would do anything his mother asked but on hot summer nights, his cravings got the best of him and he would just have to have his fix.

So, on this particular evening, our friend snuck out of the house, walked the half mile into town, past the corner where the other young men his age, (his old kindergarten nemeses) jeered and taunted him. He ignored them and headed straight for Stocker's Store. Once inside, he gave old Mrs. Stocker his money, went quickly into the side room, raised open the lid, let out a scream, bolted from the store and never touched the stuff again!

You see kind reader, Raymond's craving was for cream soda pop and when he raised the hinged lid (insulated with a rubber gasket) of the old Coca Cola cooler, he got a shock–a terrible electrical shock. Raymond ran from the store and swore off the stuff then and there!

His old school mates had set him up! 'Boots' had taken a hotshot battery and a Model T Ford coil and electrically charged the lid (rubber insulated-remember?) of the Coke cooler while Frankie and Ken kept Mrs. Stocker occupied. Raymond was a little bit deaf and did not hear the coil buzzing when he grabbed the lid of the cooler.

If you ever got a jolt from a Model T ignition, you know it's worse than a cattle fence charger. He let out a yell and threw the lid from the soda cooler right through the plate glass window of the country store. Of course, the good old boys responsible for the prank were looking in to see the fun. Mrs. Stocker gave them a 'tongue lashing' and made them pay for her window.

This story is absolutely true, and I bought that very same coil and wiring (and this story) at the household auction when 'Boots' widow sold off his stuff. I've kept that coil for sentimental reasons (I knew those big boys as responsible citizens) and because that coil might possibly come in handy, after all you never know-do you?

1927 Ford TT Truck

Some time ago, I wrote about Hank who had his late uncle's 1927 Ford TT truck squirreled away in the uncle's old blacksmith shop. It was covered with dust and several generations of junk. Everything from eel gigs, to old bed frames, to mason jars, old ladders, planet junior cultivars and stuff I could not identify. I prophesized that Hank would never, ever sell it. He was raised in the Great Depression and learned to never throw anything away—it might come in handy someday and you might not be able to afford a new one. So the Model TT huckster truck sat there for 75 years. Actually, it was originally a Hackettstown, NJ, fire truck that the uncle had modified into a covered delivery vehicle.

But I was wrong: Hank did agree to sell it, pressured by his young (younger) wife, who thought it must be worth a lot of money. It was purchased by a mutual friend of ours. I received no commission on the deal and did not have to help dig the truck out from under all the detritus. Lucky me.

Our mutual friend, Bud, bought the 1927 Huckster truck and got somebody with a roll-back to deliver it to his place. After a week or so of squirting penetrating oil into the spark plug holes and dragging it around with his Ford 4000 farm tractor, the engine freed up and he was on his way to getting it to run again.

There was an old guy from Port Murray,
Who sold his old Ford in a hurry,
Getting the title straightened out,
Without any doubt,
Caused Bud considerable worry.

A Cruise Night regular named Dilts,
Has a wife totally into quilts.
She cuts, stitches, and sews
At home and never ever goes
To car shows, to her that is totally zilch.

A special thanks to my wife of 56 years, Trudy, for putting up with me – and especially during this book project where papers are strewn all over three tables in the house.

Trudy in a hand-stitched replica of the coat found on "The Bog Man."

Trudy is a woman of many talents: one year she surprised me with her oil painting of our farm.

Oysters

You either love them or you don't. Like kittens at mice, it helps to get a taste for them while you are young as I did. We had oysters almost every week during months spelled with an R. With lot of chickens on the farm, every Friday my mother delivered eggs to housewives in Phillipsburg. So then used some of the egg money to purchase seafood at Thatcher's Fishmarket in Easton's Arcade Market.

My family had a long history of loving oysters, dating back to the 1880's. After the Bel-Del division of the Pennsy Railroad was built, the little country store in Carpentersville would get shelled oysters packed on ice in small wooden barrels. Scalloped oysters and stewed oysters made with lots of fresh milk and butter from the farm were favorites. A Frey family tradition also is oyster pie made with crushed Saltine crackers crumbs alternated with layers of oysters and butter patties, baked and served with milk. It's better than it sounds. People think you are crazy when you mention oyster pie.

It was about our second or third date. We went for a Sunday ride to High Point State Park and drove around on some back roads. We ended up at the Royal Diner #2 on Route 22. I looked at the menu and noted they had oyster stew. "Do you like oysters?" "You do?" "Me, too." The wheels began to turn as we both ordered oysters: my age, attractive, good job, home economics degree, new Plymouth…this could get serious, and it did. Pass the oysters.

Charlotte Frey's Oyster Pie
as remembered by Bob and Bruce

2 pie crusts (preferably made with lard.)

1 or 2 dozen Chesapeake oysters with salt water they have been soaking in. (aka: "oyster juice.")

Stick of real butter*

½ box of Saltine crackers.

Put pie crust in pie pan. Crush crackers and fill halfway. Add oysters. Apply a ¼ inch slice of butter on top of each oyster. Cover with remaining crackers. Add more if needed. Add half cup juice and some milk. We are not sure how much as we have never really done this ourselves. Maybe throw in some more butter. Cover with another crust. Poke some holes in crust. Bake at 350 until it looks done.

Serve in bowl with hot milk seasoned with salt and even more butter.

*National Geographic June 2017 page 138 says "add more butter!" It also says pasteurized, hydronated fats are worse than butter.

Freon Free Bull

About the best a kid could do on a hot summer day 70 years ago was to follow Second Gear Lennon's delivery truck and hope to get a few slivers of ice. There were a lot of those huckster trucks taking perishables to housewives who were busy at home keeping house, raising kids and who did not have a car.

Mr. Shackle had a 1938 Chevy Canopy Express and sold produce door to door. Mr. Hineline drove a red Ford fish monger's truck and Mr. Lennon would deliver Freon free ice which was made in an old ammonia powered ice plant.

The Frey Family had a huckster truck also. It was a 1½ ton 1917 Reo and was built like a pickup truck with the cab roof continuing on back and held up with brackets like a four-poster bed. With side curtains and benches, it became a school bus. My father (imagine this), at age 16 (and no Commercial Driver's License or insurance), hauled the township kids to high school. After graduation, my father and the Reo were relegated to farm use.

Mr. Sokoloski had a butcher shop and had fresh meat on ice all year long. He would get live animals from various farmers and would keep a 'tick' (record) of the amounts and cuts from each animal slaughtered. Then each farm family would be entitled to that much fresh meat later on from somebody else's critter. Shrink, waste, cut out and honesty also figured in to varying degrees.

Under such an arrangement, Mr. Sokoloski bargained with my grandfather for a big, old brindle bull. They tied a rope over the bull's horns, through his nose ring and fast to the right rear corner of Mr. Sokoloski's own little delivery truck, which was made out of an old Model T Ford car. They started out for town and got as far as the end of Frey's lane when the bull decided he really liked it here pretty well after all. He bucked, reared, threw back his head and overturned the Model T onto its left side. Unperturbed, my father cranked up the old 1½ ton Reo, tied the bull to it and took up the slack. They set the Ford back up on its wheels and again headed for town with the Reo pulling, the Model T pushing and a very angry bull in between. Just imagine what today's animal rights people would think! Don't tell the People for the Ethical Treatment of Animals, (PETA), please.

They finally got the bull into the slaughter pen, snubbed him down to the ring in the floor and shot him with a 22 rifle. At this point, the bull gave a mighty roar, reared up, pulled the ring up out of the cement floor, lunged for the butcher and fell over graveyard dead.

The neighbors said that the meat from that adrenalin-loaded bull was so tough that even mince pies made from that diced up meat were tough. But, at least the Frey family did not have to eat all the meat all by themselves.

Jugtown Mountain

There are a number of places everybody here knows about that do not show up on maps: Fiddlers Elbow, Hogtown and Jugtown Mountain are in my area. At one time, Jugtown Mountain was covered with apple and peach orchards (enough said). It was one and one-half miles up and one and one-half miles down the other side. There was allegedly an old still two thirds of the way up. The old Indian Trail had been widened for horse and wagon traffic. Fortunately, there was and still is a water trough which was also welcomed by truck drivers until the Interstate cut and filled the mountain roughly parallel to the old road, which was subsequently mostly untraveled.

Twenty-five years ago, I was using my 1946 Ford dump truck around the farm. I needed some fill for the barnyard so I set out on the old road over Jugtown Mountain to the shale pit. Hunterdon County, New Jersey and neighboring Bucks County, Pennsylvania have a lot of red shale. It is terrible farmland since it lays wet until June and then gets hard as a rock. It does make a good driveway material, and it's cheap.

I gave the good old boy on the Hough loader cash money, and he gave me a good six tons. I put the thirty-six-year-old Ford in low-low and ground up out of the pit. It steered very light and easy. I headed home on the old road, passed the Hunterdon Hills Playhouse and the State Police barracks, (whew), when I heard whomp, whomp, whomp. My first thought was a State Police helicopter, but then 'Bang'. The old Ford threw a rod. Chevy stove bolt sixes will run for years with a knock but flathead Ford V-8's simply will not. I coasted into a farm field so I was off the road.

Fifteen miles from home and it was milking time. I could not call home as cell phones had not been developed yet. Dick Tracy had his two-way wrist radio, but I was out of luck. What to do? I briefly considered walking back to the State Police barracks for help but I remembered I had antique car plates on the Ford. So that was a no-no. I noted a hole in the chain link fence which separated interstate 78 from the access road. I crawled through - illegal again.

Repairs were being made to the shoulder of the interstate and I jumped up on the running board of a ten-wheeler and asked the driver for a lift back to a rock quarry which was right behind our farm. For some reason, the red shale did not meet state specs. It was too cheap and too close by. The driver was the ex of a friend of the family. What luck. Soon I was home safe.

Jugtown Mountain (*continued*)

The next morning, I got log chains and clevises and my International 766 Diesel Farm tractor and headed for Jugtown Mountain. I knew I couldn't hire a wrecker to tow the old Ford home because, when raised up, the shale would spill out the back, another illegal act. And it would cost money. We hooked the tractor to the front of the truck and pulled it up to the crest of the mountain. It is illegal to tow a motor vehicle with a chain in New Jersey and the man who worked for me was not happy but he was getting paid to drive the tractor. I drove the dump truck. At the top, we unhooked the chain and hooked it to the back of the truck and to the front of the tractor and down the hill we went. This was probably illegal also, don't you think?

We made it home without getting arrested. Would I today put antique car plates and insurance on an old farm truck? Well probably, but now I would never consider towing something with a log chain on what is now a busy access road parallel to the interstate.

PS: We shoveled the red shale off the 46 Ford, transferred the body, hoist, license and insurance, etc. to a similar 1944 Ford V8 chassis and continued to use it for years. Three years ago, I sold both of them to a collector who was happy as a clam to get two good parts trucks. I was pretty happy too.

1946 European-built Ford belonging to Chris Dezwart.

A Christmas Story

It was standing-room only in the high school auditorium and we, of course, got there late. We inched our way up nearer the front and someone yelled, "Hey Bob." I looked around and so did a dozen other Bob's. Another "Hey Bob" and I spotted a friend with two seats in the front row. The big occasion was a talk (actually a monologue) by Jean Shepherd.

Those of you who remember the 1950's may recall that on cold winter nights there was little, if anything, on AM car radios, when the little stations like WKAP, WSAN and WEST shut down. All you could get were the full power stations such as Nashville, Tennessee; Wheeling, West Virginia and Cincinnati, Ohio. Thus my liking for Johnny Cash and Patsy Cline. WOR out of New York City, New York was also strong.

Talk radio back then was not all political like Rush Limbaugh, Glenn Beck and Gunther Walsh today. But on Saturday nights, Jean Shepherd was on station WOR with his humorous monologues. "Shep" preceded tall story guys like Jerry Clower, Baxter Black and Garrison Keillor by 30 years. His talks dealt with home and family life during the 1930's and eccentric people of that time period. With his dry, satirical humor he was one funny guy. For the last several years on Christmas day, one of the national TV channels has continuously run Jean Shepherd's A Christmas Story movie. It is about a kid wanting a 'Red Ryder BB gun' for Christmas, his family and their coal furnace and 1938 Oldsmobile. There were junk Model A Fords in vacant lots, kids fighting and 'double dog daring' someone else to put their tongue on an icy flagpole, Ovaltine, back alleys, coal sheds and kids bundled up in stiff snowsuits. The cars actually represent the era and a department store float was pulled by a shiny new 1939 Farmall tractor.

A good movie and every time I see it I note some new detail and as Maurice Chevalier sang in an old song, "Ah yes, I remember it well." Merry Christmas!

Two Grumpy Old Men

Gerald Kearns was our car club treasurer for years and woe be it to anybody who did not pay their dues. Jerry looked and talked a lot like Wilford Brimley, the old man in the *9 to 5* movie and in the diabetic supply TV ads. Brimley was previously a farrier by trade. Also a nice trade to fall back on.

Jerry and his wife 'Honey', had look alike 1957 Ford ketchup and cream colored hard tops and attended all of our meets. Jerry was a bit of a curmudgeon and was well into his early eighties when somebody, at one of our club meetings, made a motion that someone younger should really have access to our club's treasury account. I, being ten years younger, got the job. Jerry willingly agreed to this and one snowy winter day, I got to see a different side of the man when we spent time together at the local branch of the too-big-to-fail bank.

The armed guard opened the door for us as we entered the newly renamed Bank of America facility in Phillipsburg. It was five after two on a snowy Thursday in February. The young girl clerks were behind the counter most probably just like they had been behind the counters at 'Mickey Dees' a couple of years ago. Banks are like fast food franchises, long lines, customers waited on by people who can't make change without a computer and a manager.

The manager lady told us to have a seat as she had others ahead of us. Fortunately, the seats were soft and we struck up a conversation with the rent-a-cop. He had been placed there that day, since the bank had been robbed the day before. Not only that, but it had been robbed two weeks previously by - guess who? The same masked bandit.

Our guard informed us that he had handcuffs, a pistol and best of all, a Kevlar bullet proof vest. Jerry and I felt relatively naked. The guard was happy with the job. He normally worked in Newark and to top it off, he had a girlfriend in nearby Stroudsburg. He was happy. We all exchanged stories. Jerry told his favorite war story- the one about his adventures in Hawaii in the 1940's.

Half past two and one client left the manager's desk. An elderly couple, (even older than Jerry and me, believe it or not), shuffled up to the manager's desk, settled in and a long discussion developed; buying certificates of deposit, clipping bond coupons, setting up a trust account or discussing their health problems? We never knew. We waited. A few banking customers wandered in, looked warily around, finished their transactions and quickly left. The security cameras whirled on. Jerry and I had been on camera for at least three-fourths of an hour. Jerry produced his "Tweety-bird" squeaky toy to entertain everybody. The sheriff had neglected to search him.

The Haus Frau type manager finally told us it was our turn to approach her altar. We had to explain the reason for our visit a couple of times. We produced lots of identification. She smiled. We waited. She shuffled papers. We told her we needed to get a second officer's name added on the Lehigh Valley Regions AACA accounts. She disappeared into a back room. After a while, she returned looking worried – it was an old account.

Two Grumpy Old Men (*continued*)

She placed a phone call on a secure line perhaps, and asked for Charlotte. I don't know if she was talking to a person named Charlotte or to the corporate headquarters of the Great Big Bank of America, which is in Charlotte, North Carolina. I kid you not, I've been there.

Thus enlightened, she unlocked a closet and withdrew some papers each of which both of us had to sign several times. She explained the problem, that since it was such as old account (1986), she had to find the records. It occurred to me, that if they couldn't find the records, how did they keep track of the money, and in fact they didn't. Somebody had swiped $16,000.00 in the last two weeks from the same branch. She informed us that the Bank of America was formerly Fleet Bank, which acquired Summit Bank, which was formerly Somerset Bank and previously Phillipsburg National. We knew this. Local boys.

It was ten minutes after four when the armed guard escorted us to the door. Jerry said, 'Shoot one for me, will you?' The guard said he would and I took Jerry home to his 'Honey'. *

PS: Bank of America closed that branch in 2009.

* Jerry and his wife, Honey, were long-time members of the antique car club.

* * * * * * *

Typical Peasants

My wife and I have had the opportunity to visit Europe on geezer tours, and with a farmer's mentality I made some observations.

Land in the European Common Market has been farmed for centuries longer than the soil here in the states. They grow non-genetically-modified crops there without the use of the weed-killer Roundup.
The secret is their use of huge 24-inch by seven bottom rollover plows which bury weed seeds a foot deep and can throw the topsoil uphill.
Follow me on this circular American flow chart: The only thing politicians want to get elected (1), thus they willingly accept campaign contributions (2). One elected, politicians write laws for the Department of Agriculture and the National Resource and Soil Conservation Service (3). The USDA and NRCS discourage moldboard plowing and encourage no-till and minimum tillage to reduce erosion of topsoil (4). No-till and minimal tillage require spraying with chemicals such as Roundup (5). Roundup is made by Monsanto (6). Monsanto is a major donor to politicians (7).
Bingo – it is a full circle.

Balls O' Fire

1995 marked the 100th anniversary of the first comic strip, *The Yellow Kid*. I grew up reading the comic pages and my folks said I learned to read by reading the 'funnies'. Maggie and Jiggs, The Toonerville Trolley, The Phantom, Orphan Annie, Smilin' Jack and the Katzenjammer Kids. I particularly liked Alley Oop who was propelled through time and space by Dr. Wonmug (Einstein?). Of course, I can't forget Snuffy Smith and his 'Balls O 'Fire.'

I don't recall the Yellow Kid strip but my family did have some connection with the Yellow Kid. My grandparents had a Yellow Kid telephone twenty-five years before they had an automobile. Mr. Thomas Edison had a cement plant in New Village, NJ, and his phone line ran through my grandparents' farm. As part of the right of way agreement, my grandfather (or most likely Grandma) insisted on one of the very first telephone hookups.

According to Express Times, April 12, 1995, the Yellow Kid was originally created by R. F. Outcault, as an ancillary trademark for various Thomas Edison enterprises. Later on, it became a syndicated comic strip. Thus, the phone system was nicknamed the Yellow Kid line.

With the new phone, Grandma could talk to her sister in the city every single day, except of course, when there was a thunderstorm. During such times, random balls of fire were known to come out of that oak telephone's bakelite mouthpiece, make a U turn around the Hosier cabinet, and go right down the kitchen sink drain!

One summer evening, when the raccoons had been getting into the sweet corn, my Uncle Charlie ran into the house and grabbed a shotgun. The dogs had chased a coon up a telephone pole and it was sitting on top! Charlie took careful aim and two balls of fire came out of the shotgun and the coon fell to the ground. He ran back to the house to announce he'd got that big mama coon. Grandma cranked up the phones to tell her sister the news, but the phone was dead. How could this be? There was no thunderstorm. And then they knew! That's the honest truth, or so they told me...

Bare Tom in the Briar Patch

Our little town stretches about a mile among the Delaware River. Originally, it was the "camps" where folks from the "big" cities of Easton and Phillipsburg came out by train, pitched tents on the river bank and enjoyed swimming, boating and leisure hours. It is quite nice along the river except it does get buggy. Over the years, people built stick houses with fly netting walls and then more enclosed structures so they could enjoy the river for a few more weeks in the spring and fall. They traveled back and forth to the Raubsville, Pennsylvania side and visited friends as the Indians had done with their canoes centuries ago. Then along came Hurricane Diane in 1955 and washed the fragile structures downriver.

River people are river people the world over and rather than give up the idyllic setting, they rebuilt much more substantial structures and in the following years, the people made the river's edge their year-round home. The 1955 flood brought the people closer together. It was like an extended family up and down the river with everybody getting along just fine.

Then one year, people began to catch fleeting glimpses of somebody peering into their cabins at night. It became quite the topic of conversation and parents were afraid to let their kids play outdoors at dusk as they had always done. It just sort of ruined the fun and something had to be done - but what? There was no sense calling the police, as the town constable was sixty years old and had never caught anybody - ever.

Gradually a plan developed. They would have a great big block party at somebody's place, complete with bonfire, hot dogs, hamburgers, the whole works with all the ladies bringing covered dishes. All except one of the younger women, who bravely stayed home and donned her skimpiest outfit.

Just as it got really dark, the trap worked. Half a dozen men who had been hiding in the bushes grabbed the "Peeping Tom," threw him down, took his wallet, took off his shoes and all of his clothing and gave him back his wallet. As they led him down to the river, he was screaming for mercy. It took all six men to get him into the rowboat. When they got to the other side of the river, they hauled the terrified man out of the boat and left him standing stark naked in the briar patch between the river itself and the Delaware Canal which parallels Pennsylvania Route 611. And they were never ever bothered with a Peeping Tom again!

Remembering Luther Rherig

Our Spring Blossom Run was spoiled somewhat by the news of the death of long-time member Luther Rherig.

Luther served in World War II and after returning home, he placed an order for a new Pontiac. In the meantime, he bought, sold and traded a few cars, always turning a buck or two in the process.

In 1946, he bought a just like-new 1926 Hudson sedan, complete with little cut-glass flower vases on the inside door pillars and took his best girl to the Great Allentown Fair. The gate attendant asked him if he was an exhibitor. Luther said "No" and paid to get onto the grounds. Once inside, he realized that there was an antique car show and he could have gotten in for free.

I met Luther through a mutual friend and they helped me buy my 1917 Model T Ford. At the time (1958) and for many years thereafter, Luther had a 1914 Ford Model T Touring car that he had purchased from a Pennsylvania Dutch couple who had it stored in their living room. Luther spoke that dialect, and eventually the old couple took a 'shine' to him and sold him the car, which he kept and drove to many car shows, but none of his kids wanted that 'old thing.'

Luther owned dozens of cars in his lifetime, saved some antiques from the open hearth, was a delightful raconteur and I always sought him out at the car shows. He was a good club member, a good family man and I still miss his wit and wisdom.

In 2016, I went to the Quakertown, Pennsylvania car show and there was Luther's 1914 Ford, just like new with only a small sign of wear on the front seat. It was like meeting an old friend.

Hot, Hotter, Hottest

Although it is hot this summer, summers always have been hot in spite of what Al Gore says about American automobiles being the cause of global warming. One hot summer day eighty-five years ago my great-grandmother Charlotte set out to visit her cousin in Quakertown. They had corresponded by penny post card and cousin Emmy wrote, "Be sure to bring some elderberry jam and some pot cheese because yours taste just like what Grandma used to make." Grandma packed herself a lunch and put the things for her cousin in her wooden Longaberger style basket. She got Great Grandfather to hitch up the horse and buggy and take her to the trolley stop. (Trolleys didn't pollute but horses did!) She got on the 10am trolley. Great Grandma looked forward to these trips. She loved to watch the scenery from the high trolley car, and she enjoyed meeting and talking to people en route. Great-Grandma loved to talk.

She talked to the motorman, the conductor and other passengers as they got on board. People were friendly and made small talk. In Easton, she got off and after waiting a few minutes in the hot sun, transferred to the Bethlehem trolley. She then noticed people were not quite so friendly and looked at her suspiciously. She figured that these big city people were just 'uppity'. So she just enjoyed the scenery and the warm breezes coming through the clear story ceiling of the trolley car. It was really scorching hot when she transferred to the Quakertown Trolley in Bethlehem. The trolley was quite crowded and after she ate her lunch, she put her basket with the crocks in it under her seat. As people entered the car, they would sit down and then get up and move to the far end of the car. Eventually, she realized no one would sit near her or talk to her. Some were even standing hanging on the commuter straps and leaving seats empty near her. One woman got on, rode one block, and got off. Finally, a lady got on with a six-year-old little girl. After about one mile she pointed to Great-Grandma and said, "Pheww, Mommy. She stinks."

And so it was that my Great-Grandmother made the rest of the trip in silent embarrassment, but everybody in my family would have a good laugh about Charlotte's homemade Limburger style 'pot' cheese episode for generations.

Bob and Ruth

Bob and Ruth were born in the early part of the twentieth century. Both came from large farm families They met and married young. He got a job at a defense plant and did not get drafted in World War I. But in the subsequent recession, he got laid off. They had a couple of kids and were buying a big house in Steel City. They were liable to lose their home. What to do? After a lot of pillow talk, a solution emerged. This was before Mickey Dee's quickie breakfasts and all-night diners. Back when men carried a lunch box to work.

Ruth's mother had taught her to be an excellent cook, so it was decided to open a boarding/rooming house. She would do the cooking and washing and Bob would do everything else like washing dishes, waiting on tables, house cleaning, making beds, washing windows and tending the chickens* and the garden. So, she put an ad in the paper and put up a sign and they were in business. No zoning permits, no variances, no board of health permits and no bureaucracy to contend with.

Soon the word was out. All you could eat breakfast, a big lunch bag packed and Pennsylvania Dutch style supper every night. The rooms were full of boarders, 2 to a room, and no fighting or big Bob would throw you out. They would also serve meals to those who did not room there but paid ahead by the week. The money came rolling in. All good green money - no income tax. They soon paid off the house and starting saving.

Their kids were getting bigger and an industrial city was no place to raise a family. Both Bob and Ruth had been raised out in the fresh air on farms and were getting tired of all the industrial smoke and haze, so they sold the house and business and rented a farm. They had enough cash money to buy a used International 10-20 tractor and equipment to go with it, some milk cows, two horses and lots of chickens.

They made it through the Great Depression with hard work, plenty of good food and were happy to be out of the city. There were lots of farm sales and Bob bought better equipment, so that when World War II came he was well positioned to make some money. After the war, a nice farm came up for sale and they bought their very own place. It had been a rich man's farm with fancy buildings and nice gentle rolling fields near the river. Paradise!

They had their problems, of course, like an occasional cow dropping dead and the creamery going broke while owing them for one month's worth of milk, but they did well.

Once, while mowing hay, he accidently cut off the end of his thumb. He picked up the piece wrapped it and the thumb in his handkerchief 'snot rag' and ran to the house. Ruth put the piece of thumb in a cup of ice cubes, wrapped his hand in a towel and rushed him to the hospital where the doctors sewed in back on. With antibiotics, it healed up fine and even the doctors were amazed. Bob, however, was disgusted because the doctor had sewn it on backwards and his thumb print was now upside down.

Bob and Ruth *(continued)*

Once, while chasing the cows into the barn, the bull got after Bob. He ran for the nearby chicken house but the door was locked with a wooden pin through the hasp. He ran around the chicken house with the bull in hot pursuit and pulled the wooden pin out. On lap number two he opened the hen house door and on the third lap with the bull rapidly gaining, he jumped into the hen house and closed the door. He sold the bull and thereafter called the artificial breeder.[1]

As Bob and Ruth reached retirement age they were approached by a vitamin company that wanted their farm because of the railroad connection and mostly because of the unlimited supply of water from the underlying aquifer. Thus, they were able to retire comfortably and enjoy the 'Fruits of their Labors'. Isn't America great!

[1]Artificial breeding of cattle was introduced in America by Dr. Enos Perry of Rutgers University in 1939 and my father was one of the first farmers to use It. Embryo transplants were first done on cattle and later applied to humans: my neighbor's 40-year-old wife had triplets.

* Chickens ate the leftovers. They are dinosaurs.

International Harvester Company 10-20

Dennis and Diane

Back in the 1950s, Dennis had a job with Martz Bus Company which was expanding its routes to better compete with Greyhound Lines. The company policy was to buy up small local bus companies and integrate those routes into the Martz system.

Some of our older readers may recall that the Easton Circle was the place where the trolleys and, later on, the buses had their terminus and people could transfer in four directions. The Waer (wear and tear) Bus Company carried people to the Slate Belt area. Royal Blue coaches served southern Warren County. These were the types of mom and pop operations Martz was planning to acquire and it was Dennis's job to negotiate such deals. Thus, he did a lot of traveling and the expense account was nice.

In mid-August 1955, he was en route to Canandaigua, NY, from Philadelphia on Route 611, which was the main route. Dennis was stopped by Easton Police and told he could not travel north because of high water and flooding of the road by the Delaware River. So, he rented a hotel room and decided to get the oil changed in his car while he waited. The desk clerk suggested Cases Tire Service which was well back from the river.

On August 18 and 19, violent rains from Hurricane Diane had pelted Monroe and Pike Counties and caused serious flooding. Tragically, seventy people lost their lives and there was an unbelievable loss of property. All this water and debris funneled into the Delaware Valley where some 80,000 people lived. Many of them right along the river's edge. Of course, by now people downstream had advanced warning. But little did people realize how fast the water would rise on this sunny day. High water from the Lehigh River and the Bushkill Creek added to the flood and backed up at the Forks of the Delaware. Dennis failed to realize how close Cases Tire Service was to the Bushkill Creek.

Dennis had time to kill and watched as the floodwaters reached Easton and continued to rise, carrying all types of debris. He and hundreds of others were aghast as the 106-year-old wooden covered bridge, which had spanned the Delaware River in Columbia, NJ, was carried downstream and crashed into the steel bridge that runs from Phillipsburg to Easton. This resulted in severe damage to the 60-year-old Northampton Street Bridge. A one-hundred-foot section was completely twisted apart.

But equally tragic was all the other debris coming down the river indicating the severe loss of personal property upstream. How very sad. Dennis became aware of damage as it was occurring. Water flooded homes and businesses on Front Street. He walked around town to South Third Street and found that this was also badly flooded with lots of abandoned autos.

At least his own car was safe on North Third Street but he thought he had better check, only to find Case's Tire Store completely flooded and his new Pontiac nowhere in sight in the inundated parking lot.

Dennis and Diane *(continued)*

Dennis spent a sleepless night wondering where his car was and what to do. The following morning he found it. It was up on the lift in Case's grease bay all the while; high above Diane's waters.

PS. This is a true story as related to me by Dennis himself on a Hawaiian tour we took. Also, as a note: Case's Tire Store closed in 2000 after 90 years of continuous good service. Lafayette College recently bought Case's and the adjacent property which are both in the floodplain. Educated people aren't always too smart.

Case's Tire on North 3rd and Snyder   Buck Hall on North 3rd and Snyder

* * * * * * *

There was an old man named Bainbridge
Who lives up on the ridge
He has a path wore
Thru the rug to the floor
From sofa to the fridge

Logos and Log Chains

Most large companies have trademarks or logos that change over the years. Michelin used to have the man made from tires and now has a cute kid inside a tire. Borden once had "Elsie the Cow"; and back when you could overhaul your own car in a weekend, Hastings made piston rings that were tough but "oh so gentle." Perhaps you recall the big tough mechanic befriending a little kitten.

Joey was like the Hastings Man - gentle and kind to animals and little kids, and if you knew him, he was the roughest, toughest looking and talking young man you could imagine. Scraggly, uncombed curly hair, a week's beard, bloodshot eyes and a few missing teeth, he always made quite an impression on strangers. But his vocabulary was what was distinctive. He routinely used 'cuss' words as both adverbs and pronouns normally reserved for occasions like stubbing one's toe.

He finished high school, and as promised, his father gave him a new '48 Ford business coupe for graduation. Many a night, he entertained the locals by squealing the wheels from Gardner's Store all the way up past the Methodist Church. Eventually the coupe began to take on an appearance similar to Joey with pieces of grill and hubcaps missing. With that huge trunk, it became sort of a pick-up truck with a hinged cover over the back. They used it to haul calves to market, milk cans, hay bales—indeed anything and everything would go in the cavernous trunk. New 6.70x15 army tires were put on the rear.

One nice spring day, Joey's old man sent him out to remove some rocks that had broken the plow. So, he loaded the trunk with log chains, sledge hammers, gloves, crow bars, wrecking bars, a shovel and a couple of sticks of dynamite—in addition, he had his .22 rifle and a baseball bat behind and under the seat.

The Department of Transportation had just opened that stretch of the Interstate and Joey decided to use the new road to get to the other farm which was at the next exit. Up the entrance ramp he went with the muffler-less V8 floored. You guessed it! There was a State Police car waiting on the side of the road. Within minutes, he was surrounded by three police cars and in more trouble that you can imagine.

Moral to the story is: If I may moralize in today's politically correct society, DON'T ever carry dynamite in your old car trunk.

Missy Jane's Horse

I'm a bit reluctant to write this story and you will soon see why. It is absolutely true and is about my wife Trudy's nephew's wife - Jane.

Jane was born into one of the antebellum families in the Deep South. Prior to the Civil War, the family had slaves and grew large acreages of cotton. After the Civil War, some of the slaves left for the northern cities, some stayed on as sharecroppers and some worked for the family. These workers planted the cotton fields with loblolly and long leaf pine and Jane's family was, for a time, the largest timber landowner in Louisiana. They were also politically connected. In the disastrous flood of 1927 (much like the 2011 flood along the Mississippi), Jane's grandfather was one of the powerful men who ordered the black folks to get up on top of the levee and shovel it down by hand in order to cause a breach to save New Orleans and the rich men's properties. As Jane was growing up, her father was influential and well-known man in the Deep South. When Clark Cable came to hunt grouse, somebody took a picture of three-year-old Jane sitting on the movie star's lap.

As a teenager, Jane had her very own riding horse which was very much her pet. One day, while she was out riding, the horse stumbled, jammed a sharp tree limb into its neck and started to bleed from its jugular vein. Horrified, Jane ran to find her father, who unfortunately, was away on business. She called to Octavius and his brother who were working around the buildings. Octavius and his brother were descendants of household slaves who had worked on the plantation for generations and had elected to stay on after the Civil War. They came as fast as they could.

Octavius seized the moment and ordered his brother to quickly get a branch off a certain kind of tree and they all hurried back to where the horse lay prostrate in a pool of blood, with its eyes rolled back in its head. Octavius immediately stripped handfuls of leaves off the branch, wadded them up and placed them in the wound as a poultice. He told his brother to quickly get a pail of water and mumbled some words that Jane couldn't understand. He then said, "Don't cry Missy Jane, your horse will be ok".

When the brother got back with the water, the horse was trying to raise its' head up while Jane knelt down in the bloody mud and cradled its head in her arms. Soon, the animal was able to drink and within fifteen minutes was able to stand on wobbly legs.

These workers were originally known as Whittaker N.....s. They were imported into the southern states by someone named Whittaker who got them from Haiti. They were highly prized as household slaves. They were agreeable and happy, did not perspire, had straight black hair and they all were strangely missing their canine teeth. Each generation that worked for the family was cared for in their old age.

Jane simply could not get over how Octavius had staunched the flow of blood from her horse, and so she asked him how he had done it. He reluctantly told her it was Voodoo. This information/ability had come from Haiti with his people years ago. It had been passed down to him from generation to generation with three caveats. One was to keep it secret, two to pass the knowledge on to the next generation and three the ability had to go only to someone of the opposite sex. The problem was that there was simply no one to whom he could pass it onto. He wanted to teach Jane. He, an elderly black employee and she, a young white boss's daughter, both decided that they had better ask her pappy. Jane tried to sweet talk her father into it but his reaction was, "Hell No! I don't want my daughter growing up to be a witch and that's the end of it." Jane never forgot the horse incident and went on to be a doctor of veterinary medicine. That ancient, haunting knowledge/skill was lost to the ages.

My daughter-in-law, Sandy, on Ol' Whirlwind. My son is no dummy, but marrying her was by far the smartest thing he ever did.

The President Slept Where?

Charlie got up one half-hour early as it was his week to haul the milk for his neighbors. He milked the cows and turned them out to pasture, ate a big breakfast of bacon, eggs, and fried potatoes and finished it off with gingersnaps made with lard. He didn't worry about his cholesterol (it wasn't a health concern then) and he certainly worked off all of those calories. He loaded the warm morning milk onto his Model TT Ford Truck and then pulled the four cans of last night's milk up out of the cooling vat in the spring house, loading them also. Then he called his dog Shep, climbed in, and they were off to make their rounds. Charlie's truck had an aura all its own. It smelled like wartime alcohol antifreeze, sour milk, cigar smoke, chewing tobacco and old dog. They picked up Dink's and Obadiah's milk. The twenty-five cans made a nice load for the Model TT - eighty pounds of milk plus twenty pounds of can made over a ton.

Charlie buzzed right along with the 200-cubic engine running just below the point at which the crankshaft and main bearings started to vibrate in protest. He passed through Harmony on his way to Tranquility (I kid you not—see a New Jersey map). He was making good time this particular morning. As he came to the bottom of a hill and rounded a bend in the road, he came upon four soldiers with rifles and saw a barricade across the road. Model TT brakes were pretty good for slowing down but not much good for stopping once the brake rod clevises got worn. Charlie put both feet on the brake pedal, pulled back on the emergency brake lever and skidded to a stop. Shep rolled off the seat with a yelp and growled when the sergeant told Charlie he couldn't get through and to turn around. Charlie protested that he had to get the milk to the creamery by 10am. The soldier responded that he had better hurry and find some other route. As Charlie grumbled about spilled milk and gathered up some milk can lids, he noticed that a large locomotive with steam up was sitting on the siding with three Pullman cars hitched to it and dozens of armed soldiers standing around. "What in Sam Hill is going on?" Charlie asked, but the soldiers did not respond.

Eventually, Charlie got to the creamery by another route. There were other farmers there waiting to unload and talking among themselves. Big John, who dumped the milk cans, told them that the word was that it was the president's private train, and the Commander in Chief had spent the night at the S____ estate. The S____ family had money, old money, going back to Peter S____, who had purchased Manhattan Island from the Indians three hundred years earlier. The president traveled in the same social circle and had a friend, a close lady friend, who was also visiting the estate last night.

And so the word was out. In spite of all the secrecy surrounding the presidency during World War II and in spite of the fact that there were no fax machines, cell phones, E-mail, satellite links, Rush Limbaugh's, or Geraldo's, by noon everybody in the whole county knew where and with whom, the President of the United States had spent the previous night.

And who would have thought that this bit of scandalous information would appear in this publication.

Soybeans and Automobiles - What's the Connection?

Soybeans originally traveled to the United States by ship when Samuel Bowen smuggled them from China in 1765. But it was Henry Ford who put them in cars.

The Great Depression hit the farmers especially hard. Huge farm surpluses meant low crop prices and low income. All of a sudden Henry's best customers, the farmers, could no longer afford his cars, trucks and tractors. He knew that if there was a way out, he must find the way to do it - figure out a way to use agricultural products in industrial manufacturing and all would benefit. His chemists went to work figuring out what products could be developed from plants. Experimentation was soon rewarded with the discovery of soybean oil which made a superior auto body enamel.[1]

Soybean meal was converted to plastic that was used to make over twenty parts Including horn buttons and gear shift knobs. By 1936, Ford was using a bushel of soybeans in every car that rolled off the line. But Henry didn't stop there! While his chefs developed a variety of tasty American-Style foods from soy (including ice cream), Henry invented soybean 'wool', a fiber half the cost of sheep's wool. Soon a fabric containing 25% soybean was being used to upholster Henry's autos. Henry would even sport a suit made of soybean fiber on special occasions.

Truly, Henry was a special industrialist, but still a farmer at heart. You can take the boy off the farm, but you can't take the farm out of the boy.

Henry with sheave of grain.

Don't Throw Anything Away

Kenny's father bought a farm during the Great Depression - I'm referring to the one 70 years ago, not in 2008. The former farmer tenants could not afford to buy the farm but thought they should be given a 'break' on the price since they had lived and farmed there for several years. They were very disgruntled when they had to move. They crawled around on the beams of the barn and knocked all the wooden pins (tree nails) or trennels out of the beams, bents, and rafters that held the old Pennsylvania type bank barn together.

After Kenny's family got themselves and their animals moved in, they realized that there was nothing holding the barn together at all. Fortunately, there had been no hard winds and Kenny's father, for some reason, had saved a bunch of mortise pins from an old barn he had once helped to dismantle. Problem solved, tragedy averted. Moral to the story is, don't throw anything away.

On second thought, maybe that is not such a good idea either. I knew an instance where an elderly lady, an obsessive, compulsive hoarder, died and the mortician could not find her body amongst the newspapers, magazines, books and detritus of her lifetime.

So, if you do save everything, don't put it in, on top of, or in front of your antique car. You might not be able to get your 'Classic' out for our cruises.

Hoser Farm, Stewartsville, NJ

95

Cider House Rules

I first heard about this movie in an antique tractor magazine. A Maine collector supplied a couple of tractors for the production and, of course, they then had to hire him as a tractor consultant in as much as old John Deere's start by spinning the flywheel and are controlled by a hand clutch. He was much impressed by the attention to detail in producing a movie and the number of people involved. Actors, camera men, sound men, lighting specialist, wardrobe people, makeup artists, rainmakers with 60-foot boom trucks, people to put dust on vehicles and people to dust off vehicles and stevedores, all union, each with specific job descriptions. When he attempted to show the staff how apple boxes really should be placed in rows in an orchard, the stevedores complained that only they could move boxes. Also, he tried to point out that nobody would try to run a cider mill with a flat drive belt in the driving rain with a J.D. 2-cylinder tractor. But the director insisted that's the way it was in the book and the author of the book was producing the movie and it had to be that way. In the knife fight, there were lots of shots of Model A Fords as utility and farm vehicles. All acceptable for the WWII era.

The plot was simple, but the social and moral implications of the movie were most profound. Its rated PG is 13, and I'm glad I don't have any 13-year-olds begging to see it. The professional movie critics give this movie a high rating – a thumbs up...

but I give it a 👎

* * * * * * *

What's Black and White and weighs over 125 Pounds?

It came galloping down a half-mile farm lane when it saw the antique cars approaching. As we tried to listen to the birdwatcher's talk about open space preservation, this thing zeroed in on Charlie Miller's right leg. It was white with black spots and weighed at least one hundred twenty-five pounds. Was it a Holstein calf? Was it a space alien from the *Men In Black* horror movie that first checked out June Meyer's hinder and then was about to abduct Charlie? We will never know for sure, because a man in black sports utility vehicle came and took it away. But you people who did not make the Spring Blossom car tour missed one of the best laughs ever in the history of the Lehigh Valley AACA, for you missed the Great Dane Slobbery....

Fall Foliage Run

The bright red and yellow leaves hung really tight to the trees just for our 2002 Fall Foliage Run on November 2nd. For the last 50 years, the Lehigh Valley Region has held a tour every fall going through the scenic back roads of eastern Pennsylvania and northwestern New Jersey. Twenty-five years ago, we had as high as 50 cars in a caravan. However, times and traffic have changed. Although we only had eight cars this year, we had one of the best tours ever.

After a good breakfast at the Pennsburg Diner, our group left on a 39-mile ride through Bucks and Montgomery counties. We passed old stone farm houses, high brick Pennsylvania bank barns, prosperous dairy farms, a junk yard (or junky yard) and even some brand new "McMansions".

Our first stop was the Montgomery County Park overlooking a scenic lake, which supplies potable water to the City of Philadelphia. We then traveled to Zieglersville to the Ott Family 'Hill of Mums' which was a forty-foot high mound of dirt completely covered with blooming chrysanthemums of every known color. We toured the extensive nursery and the huge glass conservatory full of exotic ornamentals, which represented a huge capital investment. I counted a dozen "Radio Flyers" coaster wagons in daily service. Several John Deere "putt-putts" were in use as was a huge Navy surplus earth-mover tractor made by Caterpillar. Some of the men just had to crawl around on this rubber-tired monster like kids in a McDonald's playground before we left to go back to Pennsburg.

There we visited the modern Schwenkfelder Museum and Library which houses a collection of artifacts made by members of the Schwenkfelder religious group.[1] This Christian sect was persecuted in 18th Century Europe and immigrated to the area under the protection of William Penn. Schwenkfelders were and are a creative and progressive group.[2] The museum includes items of weaving, tractor art, furniture, and agricultural equipment made by members during that two centuries.

[1] It was a Schwenker who invented Locktite - a liquid which keeps bolts and nuts from loosening.

[2] Unlike the Amish

A Conversion

I'm really not much of a missionary. I have my own beliefs, keep them to myself and never try to convert anybody.

I was trying to take a nap in my 1917 Model T Ford under a shade tree at our Lehigh Valley AACA Region's 36th Annual Car Show, when I was approached by a gentleman in his 30's who had recently acquired a 1926 Ford Coupe. He had often expressed interest in the car, and when the elderly owner could no longer drive he acquired the coupe. The previous owner said, "It's yours now; you may do with it as you wish, even make a hot rod out of it, but I know the car will be in good hands."

The new owner said that he had heard that Model T Fords were hard to start, difficult to drive, unreliable, finicky, and had poor brakes; and he was planning to convert his T to a hot rod.

I said, "Crank this thing for me, and I will show you." (Model T's did not have starters until 1918). The Ford popped right off, I switched to magneto, he climbed in and off we went through the show field with the emergency brake in neutral position as I held the left pedal down to engage low gear...I pushed the spark and throttle levers ahead, opened the muffler cut out, and off we went with the engine going, "Puggidy, puggidy, puggidy," with waves and thumbs up from the crowd of show car owners and spectators. Out on Route 412, I shifted into high and opened it up, then slid the rear wheels as I braked into the local fire company parking lot.

On the way back to the show grounds, I explained the controls and extolled the benefits of the Model T - the 'Universal Car' as Henry Ford's PR people promoted it years ago.

Back under my shade tree there were two happy men: the younger guy had made up his mind to keep his Model T Stock, and I, at 80 years of age, had made my first conversion, a non-conversion.

Towing a T with an M after conversion to electric start. Note chain.

The 'Bootleg' Mine

Cold weather is here, Already this winter, I've seen a lot of oil delivery trucks parked on the city streets with the poor driver dragging a stiff red hose. One thing we do not see much of is coal trucks. There was one in Riegelsville a few years ago and one was parked on RT 309 north of Route 78 and south of Orefield recently. Coal delivery trucks were dump trucks with special sub frames that rose with a scissors-like parallelogram. Once the whole body was raised up 10 feet or so, the coal could be dumped down chutes and through cellar windows into basement bins. Some houses in town were not thus accessible, and the driver had to carry the coal in heavy canvas bags down cellar steps or through the house.

Our neighbors, the Snyder "boys" (actually young married men) worked very hard on their father's farm. The father was a task master and a perfectionist. The crops were well-cultivated and the buildings well-painted, but he did not pay the 'boys" very much.

In order to support themselves, they bought a used 1925 Model TT Ford dump truck with a hand lift and a Warford auxiliary transmission. After the farm chores were all done, Donald would grab a sandwich and head for a "bootleg" * coal mine outside of Tamaqua. It was a long bumpy ride. He would load up 2-1/2 tons of chestnut coal from the hopper, pay the guy cash and head home. The Warford transmission had an overdrive and an underdrive, thus giving six speeds using the two-speed planetary foot-shifted stock transmission. Donald would get home and catch some sleep, hopefully before it was time to get up and milk the cows again.

The following night Harold would service the truck and head east to towns as far away as Somerville and Highland Park. He would knock on doors until he found somebody who needed coal, had an accessible cellar window and - most importantly – cash money. The latter was most important since this was in the middle of the Great Depression. Harold would then return home and get some sleep.

One night, Harold was coming home empty and missed his shift on the Warford and could not get it double-clutched back into gear. He was descending the west side of Jugtown Mountain (now Route 173), and with the auxiliary transmission in neutral he had no transmission brakes at all. He rode it out and because of the inherent friction in the worm drive rear end and the external contracting rear brakes, he made it down the hill safely but coasted halfway to Bloomsbury.

*A 'bootleg' or gypsy mine was a small usually family owned and operated business. It was not associated with and in fact was despised by the major coal and railroad corporations which pretty much had a monopoly on coal.

A 'Geenus' was a Genius

Horace was a 'geenus' according to my grandmother. A 'geenus' was a genius. In Horace's case, perhaps not a genius as defined by Webster, but surely a smart, gifted and talented man who could and would tackle anything. In his eighties, he laid a stone foundation and worked on his barn roof.

Horace was a farmer, and during World War II he was unable to get any hired help so he designed his own manure cleaner. He took an old horse-drawn McCormick mowing machine, removed the cutter bar assembly and belted up an electric motor to the Pitman wheel. He replaced the original drive wheels with heavy sprockets and a chain mechanism. This ran a reciprocating arrangement in the cow manure 'drop' which dragged the muck out of the barn and dropped it into his manure spreader.

A farm machinery salesman (with nothing to sell during the war) heard about Horace's invention, stopped, and later returned with an engineer from James Mfg. Company. Horace proudly operated his device, and after the war thousands of Jamesway manure cleaners were sold to farmers nationwide. AND - you guessed it - Horace never got one red cent. We locals called it "The Horace Way."

Sleep Cheap

Sometimes they stayed in campsites, sometimes in relatives' back yards and sometimes in Grange hall parking lots. The two kids slept on the front and back seats. The parents slept in sleeping bags on the grounds under a canvas draped over the roof of their 1953 Chevy Biscayne, with one side slammed in the car doors and the other tied to a step ladder. The daily menu consisted of dry Wheaties, a loaf of bread, two quarts of milk, some peanut butter and one-half pound of baloney. The main meal was canned tuna and noodles on a fold-up Coleman stove.

Gypsies, you ask? Hardly, just good parents who felt their children should be exposed to the scenic wonders and historical points of interest in America while they were still part of the family unit.

Before they knew it the kids were grown and gone and when the parents traveled they stayed where Tom Burdett kept the lights on for them and they lived on value meals. Mother had always wanted to visit the Big Apple and they guessed maybe they could finally afford to stay just one night at the Waldorf Astoria Hotel and to dine at the very proper British Bull and Bear Restaurant therein. So she booked the room.

They grudgingly paid through the nose for parking in the Big Apple but they were determined not to let that spoil their day. They went to the Empire State Building and shopped at Lord and Taylor and at Saks Fifth Avenue. They did not buy anything though, as there was nothing that they really needed and frankly they felt a little uneasy in the posh surroundings. So they held hands like lovers, looked at everything and hoped they wouldn't look too much like Country Bumpkins.

Finally, it was time to check in at the Waldorf. Ah yes, the lobby was as impressive as they had always head it was, with marble floors and colonnades, polished walls of mahogany inlaid with rosewood, art deco lights and of course the imposing front desk.

Check-in went off without a hitch. They held onto their overnight bags so that they wouldn't have to tip the bellhop who hovered over them while they waited for the elevator to arrive. It seemed like an eternity. Once inside they breathed a sigh of relief.

After freshening up they went back down to the 'Bull and Bear' for high tea. It took a while to get their eyes adjusted to the dark as the tuxedo clad waiter led them to their tiny table set with solid silver. They noticed the huge black walnut timbers and stained-glass windows and leaded glass light fixtures. The décor was right out of a medieval castle. The waiter brought scones and they ordered Earl Gray tea with cream. Tiny glass jars held a variety of jams, jellies and marmalades. One teaspoon out of a jar and the solicitous waiter brought another. Such class, such elegance. The Brits had a good idea with tea time. Ah, this was the life. They tipped fifteen percent.

They went back to the car to get the rest of their stuff. He somewhat reluctantly carried the iron and ironing board and she carried the bag with some food for their supper. They knew they couldn't afford to eat at Club 21, so they brought some stuff from home to eat in their room.

The door man opened the gold-trimmed two-inch thick plate glass doors for them, and right in the center of the cavernous lobby the over ripe tomatoes and cantaloupe fell out of the bottom of the bag. The husband bent over to help her scoop up the mess and dropped the ironing board with a clatter. All the blue-haired dowagers ensconced in the brocaded armchairs looked aghast. Uniformed staff rushed into clean up the mess as the couple rushed to the elevator. They studied the embossed stainless-steel doors again while they waited another eternity for the elevator to come. Once in the safety of their room, they had a good laugh. They changed their clothes, slunk out of the Waldorf to do the town, see the bright lights, and grab hot dogs from a street vendor before a good night's sleep in the best of Americas five-star hotels.

True story as told by the lady involved.

Soft seats...sleep cheap.

Out West They Used to Shoot Horse Thieves

The Greenwich Vigilante Society was organized in 1812 with the purpose of apprehending horse thieves and mutually insuring horses, mules, and stolen carriages. The area covered was all of southern Warren County and northern Hunterdon County, New Jersey.

All was well until 1882, when two horses and a wagon disappeared. We don't know if any lawsuits were threatened, but we know the society paid the secretary to go to Belvidere and Trenton. Also, they paid lawyer W. M. Davis $23.50 for incorporation papers. Total assets of the society were $815.42 (probably $15,000 in today's dollars).

There were 77 original members paying $5.00 each. The membership could be transferred to another in their lifetime or inherited.

After reorganizing in 1882, the first business was to reimburse Mr. Barber $200.00 for his horse. Then they paid the expenses of the pursuers, a detective, and a Mr. Mettler for his horse and wagon, bringing the treasury down to $131.22. They never again paid for property loss but later paid to help find Mr. Slight's horse.

By 1919 when the treasurer reported a balance of $24.57, there was a request by Mrs. Walker* to insure automobiles. The directors talked it over and thought it could be done but voted against going into automobile insurance. Secretary of the organization in 1919 was Isaac Hance, Bob Frey's grandfather.

In 1920, Isaac Hance bought a Star automobile. Thus ends the written history of the Greenwich Vigilante Society, as found in the attic of Frey's farm house.

* Mrs. Walker was the wife of the Old Greenwich Presbyterian Church minister.

Upsot

I finally became "Grandpaw" a couple of years ago. The Frey generations are pretty far between. I had pretty much given up on the idea, but I am pleased to say I now have an excuse to play with Tonka toys in a sandbox. Time thus spent has given me pause to think about my own Grandpa.

His first car was a 1917 truck...a Reo Speedwagon. It was a station wagon (now called Crossovers) with a wooden body on a one-ton truck chassis. The Reo made a very utilitarian farm vehicle, but it wasn't a very fancy thing in which to go to church. It also served as a school bus as my father, at age sixteen, hauled all the township kids to the local high school with no bus driver license, no CDL, and probably no insurance. Just Imagine!

By 1937 the Reo was junked, and my grandfather bought me a very nice metal (Tonka) toy dump truck with the four dollars he got from the sale of the Reo. I used this toy truck hard in my very own sandbox which was a reconstruction project in a water drainage ditch. I no longer have the toy truck or the 1917 Reo - and it would be nice to have them both - but I've got more than enough 'stuff' at this stage of my life so I'm quite content with memories of Grandpa.

These include napping in his arms in church, of ice cream cones, horse races at the county fair, trips for baskets of early peaches, of kite flying and of old "Dewey".

Dewey was a plug work horse that I was allowed to ride. He was really old and Grandpa probably kept him for sentimental reasons. I never knew why they named him Dewey, but it occurred to me it was because he was so slow that the dew settled on him, but most likely he was named for famous Admiral Dewey of the Spanish American War and not for the 1940 presidential candidate, who was younger than the horse.

One Christmas vacation we had a lot of snow, and I got it into my adolescent mind that it would be nice to take a real Currier and Ives sleigh ride. I don't know if it was my idea or if Grandpa put it into my head, but he and I unloaded all the accumulated junk out of the sleigh, got the sleigh down out of the mow with block and tackles, got the shafts down out of the rafters and got old Dewey harnessed and hooked up between the shafts. We even put sleigh bells around the horse's neck. Grandpa gave me detailed instructions and I was off on my solo flight. At this time, no one had thought of using road salt. The cars had packed the snow down nicely, and Dewey had been recently shod. Smooth sledding.

I went a mile down to our little village to "show off" and to see if any of my buddies wanted to go for a ride, but nobody was around. So I went to the home of a classmate and asked her if she wanted to go for a ride. She smiled, got her coat and mittens, and I helped her up into the sleigh and away we went, My first date.

All went well until I attempted to turn right onto Winter Road (I kid you not) and just like the song "Jingle Bells" we "upsot" the sleigh, and my little blonde friend and I ended up in a snow bank. Fortunately, nobody was hurt, and the horse stood still while we struggled to right the sleigh. By then I realized why Grandpa told me to go slow on corners. A sleigh does not turn like an airplane or bicycle. It just slides and skids around because it is rigidly attached to the horse with the shafts (poles) so that it will spin out on turns like a midget race car on a dirt track.

By this time the horse decided it was time to head home, and since we were wet and cold we figured it was a pretty good idea. Marilyn held the reins while I slid the sleigh around. We both jumped in and headed back. So much for my first date.

The next day Grandpa and I put the sleigh back upstairs in the wagon house, and it is still there with almost 60 years of junk piled on top of it. I don't recall if I ever thanked my Grandpa for the experience, and I probably did not. But if my grandkids ever show a similar interest, I'll dig that sleigh out in a minute. Trouble is... I don't know where I will keep a horse. But do you know what? I'll find a place!

Ready Mix

Ray grew up on a farm and always wanted to farm for himself but circumstances did not permit it. So, he got a job at a local fertilizer plant. He was like the guy on the "Dirty Jobs" television show who would and could tackle anything. He also retained some of that inbred arrogance that farmers get through the nipple and possessed the peasant's disdain of authority.

The manager of the fertilizer plant put Ray to work driving a big truck that spread lime and fertilizer. It was not like farming where the soil, (sand box) equipment (toys) animals (pets) and home (castle) are your very own (and the PNC banks) and you can do as you very well please. Still, the job was interesting and he got to talk to a lot of farmers as he made deliveries and listened to them gripe.

He had a bad morning bouncing across corn rows and the wet lime (which has the consistency of fine damp sand) kept bridging up. Every time this happened he had to get out of the cab, climb up into the nine-foot-high body and shovel. His back hurt, and he had two more loads that day.

When Ray got back to the fertilizer plant one of the other spreader trucks had a broken rear axle shaft. The boss told Ray to fix that guy's truck and asked the guy to take Ray's truck and deliver the 13-ton load.

Ray wolfed down his lunch, got his tools and started to work. It was a down on the knees in the gravel with a damp northeast wind in the face job. Big trucks have full floating axles which drive but do not carry load as do light duty pickups. He got the big end of the axle out easily, but the small piece eluded him. It was sort of like trying to snare a rubber chicken in a wine bottle in the pitch dark.

It was 4:30 when Ray got the new axle in and bolted up, put his tools away and got his hands cleaned up. At this point the boss appeared and told Ray to load up another load of lime and spread it. Instead of explaining to the manager that his back and knees were killing him and that he would come in early tomorrow to do it, he just said "I quit" and stalked off.

Ray had no trouble finding another job at the ready-mix cement plant. He already had his commercial driver's license from when he worked at the fertilizer plant and the job was close to home. It was an interesting job going to construction sites, seeing how buildings were built and watching the interaction between the bosses of the works and building inspectors. Once in a while he would get the ten-wheeler really stuck, and they would have to get a bulldozer to get him out. Great fun.

One day he got to make a delivery to the local chemical plant and as he backed his way through the storage yard using his mirrors, the hydraulic pump that sticks out about a foot beyond the front bumper hit a gallon jug on a pallet. The yard man who was directing Ray got on the cell phone immediately and then disappeared. A big klaxon (Oogah-oogah) horn went off and sirens wailed. Men came running, stumbling as they tried to don their white plastic coveralls and put on boots. More people

Ready Mix (*continued*)

with their Hazmat paraphernalia poured out of the office building. Ray kept the mixer running so the cement would not set up. Then the town police and emergency squad showed up, followed by the fire company. Ray was surrounded by shouting worried looking people, some with cell phones, some with cameras, some with pencils and pads, some yelling orders and some running off on command. The sirens continued with hardhats everywhere.

When the State Police arrived, Ray figured Lisa Jackson, head of the New Jersey Department of Environmental Protection, was probably on her way to the spill site. So, Ray shrugged his shoulders, got down out of the Mack Truck cab, and said to the State Police, "Alright put the handcuffs on me and take me away."

About that time a burly worker arrived with a 50-pound bag of speedy-dry (cat litter), poured it on the puddle, and everybody wandered off and went back to work. When Ray told his new boss, he expected to get fired again, the boss just laughed and laughed.

* * * * * * *

Where Have all the Brass Cars Gone?

Where have all the brass cars gone?
Long time passing,
Gone to tarnish every one.
Where has all the tarnish gone?
Long time passing,
Gone to silver, everyone.
Where has all the silver gone?
Gone to sporks everyone.
Where have all the sporks gone?
Long time passing,
Gone to landfills every one.
When will they ever learn?
When will they ever learn?

With a bow to Peter, Paul and Mary

Rode Hard...Springs...

It is funny how stories come together, and I hope I do not lose you here. By chance I ran across an old issue of the AACA Magazine, and in it was a typical story about someone who found and restored a big 1920 Packard which had belonged to Bethlehem Steel CEO Charles Schwab. My father-in-law once owned a 1920 Packard which he bought new and traded in his 1914 Oldsmobile. He hardly ever got rid of anything, but he did get rid of that touring car.

January 1920 was bitter cold when his wife Sarah had a baby girl. She and the child were kept in the Philadelphia Hospital for two weeks as was the custom 85 years ago. And the doctors would not allow them to be brought home in Bruce's open touring car. He had to hire a taxi cab for the occasion. He soon decided that he really should have an enclosed family car. Thus, he bought the Packard. It was used only to go shopping, to church and occasionally to the shore to visit relatives. Typically, on such trips Sarah sat in the back seat, filed her nails and went to sleep. But she never liked the Packard: she said it rode hard. Bruce, from his front seat, thought that the car rode and handled well and it certainly had lots of power on the hills. Eventually the Packard was traded off on a DeSoto.

Back to the AACA article about the details of restoring Schwab's 1920 Packard. In it the owner mentioned that they had discovered that the rear seat springs were still tied down with webbing, just as it came from the factory. Bingo! That's why Sarah said that their Packard rode hard. The springs on it were also tied down. Probably both the 1914 Olds and the family 1920 Packard became open hearth material for Schwab's Bethlehem Steel mill furnaces.

But wait. There is more to this Lehigh Valley story. As a retirement gift, the Bethlehem Steel Board of Directors gave Charles Schwab a brand new 1939 Cadillac convertible. When Schwab passed away the attorney and executor of the sizeable estate contacted his personal friend Victor Banas who acquired the convertible for a song. "Vic" and his wife Anna were long time members and attended many meets in their 1939 Caddy. Hopefully that car escaped the crusher and might still be in the valley. If anybody knows about that car let me know. It might make yet another convoluted story.

My mother-in-law sitting on the right front door of a 1914 Model T.

Maple Syrup and Sweet Corn

In spite of Al Gore's man-made global warming, we did have some real winter weather this winter just before Christmas - remember? There still are some mighty cold places in the lower 48. Colder than Sarah Palin's capital of Juneau that never gets colder than 30 degrees Fahrenheit. Bismarck, ND is one cold place as is Mount Washington, NH where they have the weather station secured with a log chain so it won't blow away. (I kid you not.) Not too far away is Stoddard, NH and occasionally that is the coldest place.

Stoddard has its own digital twenty-first century US Government weather station mounted on a tree stump in Charlie Strickland's backyard behind his small New England style white clapboard house. Charlie is in his late eighties and his place is right out of the 1700's. He has a wood pile the size of a box trailer ready to heat the house and fuel his maple syrup evaporator. Of course, there are a couple of modern things. He does have electricity, and his sons bought him a John Deere 'Gator'. He now uses the Gator to harvest sap every spring from maple trees scattered around town. But he did keep his donkey which he takes for a walk down town every day and visits with the locals. Charlie has absolutely the thickest New England accent I've ever heard and (like Bob Frey and his silver queen sweet corn) he is too proud to sell his maple syrup. He just gives it away - if he likes you. Incidentally, Stoddard, NH is the town made famous in the photos and paintings of the three white churches reflected in a mill pond. (Actually, one is the town hall and one is the community hall). So, if you ever see the picture I'm referring to, think of good ole Charlie Strickland and progress.

Real maple syrup is delicious on corn fritters made with fresh sweet corn.

* * * * * * *

1888

The snow was gone and turned to mud. April first was universal moving day for all the tenant farmers who had been evicted or were trying to better themselves by moving to another place. Isaac and Charlotte Frey and their kids had been living and farming along the Brunswick Pike*. The children walked to school which was in the small brick building that is still standing across US Route 22 West from Straw Church. **

The Freys had packed up all of their household goods which amounted to a cook stove, table, chairs, dishes, canned goods, potatoes and hams. It was customary for the moved farm family to feed the neighbors who had helped them move, so the wagon with the household things had to go first. A couple of the men and most of the women and girls went first to set up the stove. It was two and a half miles to the Mixsel Place, located three fourths of a mile east of Carpentersville. It was known as the 'soup bean' place. It had 134 acres, a run-down house, a thirty-four by sixty-foot frame Pennsylvania style bank barn with a four-foot overshot *** and the corn crib.

After the rest of the neighbors arrived with extra wagons they started to load the farm goods, hay, corn and oats. The children had great fun catching the chickens and putting them in crates. Pigs were crated and heaved onto a wagon. A halter was put on the bull with the rope running through his nose ring and tied to the rear of the wagon loaded with hay. The children went ahead to open and close fence gates along the proposed route.

And so, they were off with the hay wagon and bull tied behind, leading the way with cattle following and being herded by the teenagers. The cattle had not been fed that morning in hope that they would follow the hay wagon. The other wagons and men followed. They had to pass over the Jersey Central, under the Lehigh Valley Railroad, and onto the old Indian trail that passed the Mixsel Place. Finally, they got the cattle into the barnyard which had a stone wall around it and the pigs into the pigpen. There were ten cows, three horses, three little pigs, walking plows, hay rake, cultivator, sleigh, and stone boat were on the other wagons.

* Now Route 122, south of Phillipsburg, NJ.

** Straw Church is so-named because the original Lutheran Church had a thatched roof.

*** Overshot is an overhang on the south side. It was nice and warm under there in the winter and cool in the summer, because it was shaded.

1888 continued...

All of a lifetime's possessions[1] including bedding and furniture had to be unloaded and put where Charlotte wanted it. Oats in the bin, hens in the hen house and the dog tied to the dog house. The men shoveled the ear corn into the crib and forked the hay into the haymow, and with perfect timing one of the women yelled, "DINNER!"[2]

The men all washed their hands and faces in the same basin with the same block of homemade soap and dried off with the same towels made from feed sacks. The little kids had been fed first and chased outside. When the men were seated Ike said "grace," thanking the good Lord for a good day, good neighbors and a good life. Then plates were passed around with home-canned corn, pickled eggs with sour beets, baked potatoes, noodles with lots of butter, coleslaw, home-smoked ham with lots and lots of gravy on homemade bread. Dessert was apple pie with the crust made with lard.[3]

Conversation covered incidents of the day, gossip, and lots of kidding of each other. Soon it was time to go home because the neighbors had chores to do at home. Their consensus was that the Freys would not last a year on that poor farm. But 129 years later, we are still here.

1. Both then and now, people have a lot of stuff.
2. "Dinner" was at noon. "Supper" was in the evening.
3. Yum-yum. Really good pie crust. Lard probably isn't any worse for you than hydrogenated palm oil.

* * * * * * *

ROY THE BIG BOY

Like a kid in a big sandbox, Roy farmed land in two counties. He saw an ad in the weekly *Lancaster Farmer* and purchased a used John Deere 4010 to be delivered by the seller on a certain day. The terms agreed upon were that Roy would pay the gentleman by check, and the man could cash it at the local (Bloomsbury, NJ) bank.

At 9 am, Roy went to the bank and transferred a sufficient amount of money from his savings to his checking account. The man unloaded the tractor; Roy gave him a check and told him that he could cash it at "his" bank a mile down the road.

Fifteen minutes later the man was back, angrily saying: "The bank won't cash your check."

Roy jumped into his beater truck, tore down to the bank, and asked: "Where is Benner?"

"Oh, Mr. Benner is in conference and is not available."

Roy stormed into the office, grabbed the bank president by the collar and asked what the _ _ _ _ had he done with Roy's money. The bank officer explained bank policy and overnight float...and then quite wisely honored Roy's check.

(See also page 183)

Scoop

Sometimes in farming you end up with a piece of equipment left in the field somewhere. It is hard to explain - it just happens. Somehow our old 1970 Dodge Pickup got left back on a long lane for a while. It was not one of the famous Power Wagons. It was a ½ ton four-wheel drive wide-bed and it had more than its share of hard use and of problems. It had a birdbath hood with concave areas that held rain water until it evaporated or somebody moved the thing. We called it the "Pumpkin Wagon" because it was painted a faded-out orange and sat around for extended periods. I had forgotten where I left it.

One mid-summer evening after eating supper and after a brief rain-shower with a cold front moving in, I went out to mow alfalfa. I met two guys with big grins on their faces coming out of that private lane. Their expressions changed when they realized they could not get past the nine-foot-wide haybine and that I had the tines of the mounted front-end loader on my International 656 tractor lined up with the grill of their pickup.

I figured they were back in the lane drinking beer and throwing out the bottles. It did not immediately occur to me that they might be on drugs and might be violent. I felt I was in control of the situation and started in on a lecture about property rights when I realized my Pumpkin Wagon was loaded with something black, so heavily that the back bumper was almost on the ground.

I pocketed the key to the 656, set the brakes, left the scoop bucket resting on their Ford Truck bumper and went to examine my old Dodge.

I found out what these guys had been laughing about minutes earlier: they had apparently stripped an old slate roof and had intended to dump the slate, lath and nails back in my field, but they came up on the ultimate practical joke of transferring it all to my Pumpkin Wagon.

By that time I was really hot. I demanded their driver's licenses or I would completely demolish their pickup including squashing the cab. It turned out that neither one had a license, and the truck belonged to the driver's brother. They were visibly upset when I threatened to call the police. I did not have a cell phone. (Today I finally have one.) So we struck a deal: they were to reload their pickup from the stuff on my truck - every single flake of slate, lath and every last nail, take it to a landfill and be back the next day with the weigh slip from the land fill. Otherwise, I would take their truck license number to the local cops, and both guys and their brother would be in serious trouble. It worked because they were back at 10 am apologizing profusely, with the slip in hand and I never saw them again.

112

Jake

Although he had always lived close by and although we had friends in common, I never knew Jake until about twenty-five years ago. At that time, his sons (as young motor heads) spent a lot of time working on, racing and then fixing little Austin Healy 'Sprite' sports cars in Jake's garage and on his lawn under Jake's scrutiny.

Jake worked for years as Maintenance Supervisor for the town housing authority. Thus, he had the facilities as well as the abilities to do almost anything. He was, however, in a bit of a rut; got up, grumbled, went to work, came home, ate, watched TV, went to bed, got up, grumbled, etc. Somewhere along the line, he acquired a 1929 Model A Ford coupe in pieces - a real basket case if there ever was one. I had and still have (but that's another story) a similar intact Model A, and Jake would visit and scrutinize things. Anyone who knew Jake would attest to his ability to scrutinize things.

As work progressed on his Model A, he would work late in the evening, get up early in the mornings and work on pieces during his lunch break. Using my parts as patterns, he even fabricated new drip edges and repro trim parts from sheet stock. He subscribed to *Hemmings Motor News* *, scrounged up needed parts, bought two or three for spares and stored them away along with a lifetime's accumulation of other stuff that just might come in handy someday. This was not an aberration - it was simply what a frugal person did if he had lived through the Great Depression and had the room to squirrel stuff away.

I invited Jake to go along on our 1975 Fall Foliage Tour. We visited Hope, NJ, where the women heard a presentation by the Hope Historical Society and the men visited Stew Johnson who had even more junk squirreled away than Jake did.

Jake and his wife joined AACA and the Lehigh Valley Region as soon as the restoration was complete, and they hardly ever missed a club function. Grace was always smiling and visiting with the club ladies with Jake scrutinizing. She liked parades and loved to decorate the Model A. They have both passed away now, but they had fifteen years of enjoyment out of that little Model A coupe and made a lot of friends of which I'm proud to have been one.

* a monthly automotive magazine

Silver Creek

The 1997 Silver Creek Show was a success and was better than ever. Although I like music of the 40's, 50's and 60's, it was nice to spend the day in a quiet park with only an occasional bit of stack music.

Registration went well thanks to Honey and Jerry Kearns and their team of helpers. The AACA goody bags and their contents gave entrants the impression that the Lehigh Valley Region is indeed a good club.

It was a nice idea to have the participating car dealers give trophies to the best of their marquee. Personally, I liked the 1951 Chevy two-door Skyline which was meticulously restored in metallic green. The styling of these slope-backed Chevys is very similar to the 1954 Bentley coupes that bring $150,000 now and also to 2017 cars in general.

Speaking of styling - that little maroon and black Citroen really stole the show. Like Barbara Streisand, it's so unsightly that it's pretty. It was France's 1948 answer to Germany's VW bug. The roof and side window treatment reminds one of an egg.

The raffle for the car drivers was a nice idea and a complete success. It was a lot of work for our President Joe and his family to solicit the prizes from various businesses, and we thank them all for the donations. The raffle really did hold the crowd's interest.

The absolute highlight of the day was when our editor's ticket won her a coupon to get her front-end aligned. Enough said!!

Foggy Thoughts

There was a man who did jog,
Every morning in the fog,
He really felt great,
But it was his fate,
To get squashed like a groundhog.

There was an old geezer named Ken,
Who just waits for the week end,
When he goes to line dances,
And with all the pretty young women he prances,
And will prance to the very end.

There was a man signed up with Uber
With his 1940 Buick Super
It's really not funny,
He is trying to make money
But he is in southern Cubar

Old Maytag's with one-cylinder engine,
Washed clothes to perfection
New ones even with soap
Wind bib overalls up like rope
Which really gets under my skin

There once was a man name Dunn,
Who thought it was much fun,
To knock down bee's nests,
And it was quite a test
To see how fast he could run.

Repro Rocky Mountain Brakes

On June 13, 2003, my son Rob and I took off from Lehigh Valley International Airport through cloudy skies and got to Dearborn, Michigan, just as it cleared up there.

We had planned to trailer our 1917 Model T Ford to Ford Motor Company's 100th Anniversary celebration. Bernie Hank (one of the founders of our Lehigh Valley AACA Region) who had restored the car, drove it to Dearborn for Ford's 50th. He later sold it to me since his wife refused to ride in it ever again. In 1978, we trailered the Model T to Dearborn for Ford's 75th Festival and got a trophy. It's hard to believe but it was the only 1917 on the show grounds.

We signed up #1922575, manufactured June 1917, and started to get ready six months ahead of time. My wife by now was refusing to ride in the Model T also, and somehow heard about Rocky Mountain Brakes from, I believe, Dora Serfass. Rocky Mountain Brakes were an extra after-market accessory back in the Model T's heyday. They were an external contracting band brake system, which was designed to supplement Ford's three-pedal transmission internal brake. Repro Rocky Mountain Brakes were available, and I ordered a set.

Not being one to let things well enough alone, I ordered modern bearings and grease seals to upgrade the rear axle since Model T Fords, mine included, tend to leak grease if indeed there is any grease in the rear end, but it looked like somebody had shelled walnuts in the 'punkin'. This was due to the fact that Model T's had an inherent weak point in the thrust bearings on the rear axles. For a vehicle designed in 1906 and 1907 the Model T was remarkably modern. The thrust washers were made of babbit or some other odd mixture of lead and tin that was about like 'pot metal' and the thrust washers tend to fail. Modern repros use modern metallurgy, but the reproduction wheel bearings were, hard as this is to

believe, tight on the 86-year-old axle shafts. What to do? What to do?

Back to the junk pile and I dug out another rear axle, which had at one point been somebody's two-wheel cart. I have not the faintest idea how or from whom I got it, but I had it. It yielded two good old roller bearings. (I had two good ones in my original axle) plus a couple of gears that I needed. Lang's Company supplied other parts as needed, but the bronze bearing for the torque tube needed machining and that took a month for the guy to get around to doing it. And so we ordered airline tickets to Ford's 100th Bash.

Ghost of Christmas (Parties) Past

Several holiday seasons ago we returned home from our Antique Car Club Annual Christmas Party at Alice and Ed Dietrich's house only to hear water running. A trip down to the cellar revealed that the hot water heater was leaking, and the water was ankle deep and lapping at the oil burner unit. It turned out that the float on the sump pump had gotten stuck, and the water was mighty cold.

Fast forward to the Region's Christmas party in December 2012, and I had another problem in the cellar. One of the two interconnected fuel oil tanks was going drip-drip-drip. A five-gallon pail half full of speedy dry under the drip kept the cement floor from becoming saturated but... what to do with the leak? Off Trudy and I went to the feast at the local eatery, and I consulted with a half-dozen knowledgeable gear heads. The consensus was that probably the thick stick kind of JB Weld[1] was the best thing to try. Meanwhile back home my younger son, who lives in that house, came to the same conclusion and kneaded up a glob of JB Weld and pressed it hard into the area of the leak and it stuck. Alas, the metal in that area was so porous that the leak was now drip-drip-drip-drip. In panic, he tried an aerosol bomb of Rustoleum black elephant snot designed to seal leaks in rainspouts, shingles and slate roofs. He sprayed it liberally. But the #2 furnace oil diluted the aerosol tar, and it just drip-drip-drip-dripped faster. Next, he mixed up some 'Bondo', smeared it around and fastened the fiber glass mesh with good old gorilla tape (souped-up duct tape), and "Whoopee"- the leak was back to drip-drip-drip. Slow enough that it would not (hopefully) fill the five-gallon pail overnight.

Son Rob and I slept rather fitfully, fearing what would happen if the cellar got flooded with number two heating oil. Come morning we found that the patches held, and I borrowed my neighbor's (A.C. Hartung – he owned a maroon 31 Buick rumble seat roadster) five-hundred-gallon farm weed sprayer and transferred the oil out of both sixty-year-old fuel tanks. I am not endorsing or condemning any of the products we used, but they worked; and if you have any sixty-year-old fuel tanks in your cellar, you are on your own. Don't call the Freys, whatever you do.

[1] JB Weld is a metal- patching product of playdoh consistency that hardens.

Remembering Saturday Nights

Bob Stecker's Esso Station served all the usual automotive functions, and in addition it was the unofficial community center on Saturday nights. Old Timers with nothing better to do and kids with only bicycles to drive would gather, and older kids with cars would cruise around some and then drop by and watch the action.

During the summer months Dorney Park offered stock car races. Modified 37 Fords regularly ran on Saturday nights, and occasionally late model Hudsons, 1949 Fords, Plymouths and Oldsmobiles would battle it out on the tiny quarter-mile track with tires squealing. But year round, it was almost as much fun to sit around on soda crates at Stecker's Esso and watch the fun, and it was FREE.

Everybody went out on Saturday nights - to the movies, perhaps, drive-ins, car hops, hot dog stands, saloons, night clubs, fire halls and most of them at some point went around Straw Church circle too fast. The local traffic mixed in with the New Year drivers who had survived the Ledgewood and Somerville circles prior to the interstates.

Some now retired New Jersey Highway engineer had figured that the secret to efficient traffic flow through intersections was the traffic circle, with automobiles entering at a tangent. Perhaps he had encountered Easton, Pennsylvania's Center Square or knew about England's roundabouts. Anyway, with nose-heavy cars of the 1950's and 60's and bias ply tires, Saturday nights at the Esso was the place to be...especially when somebody did not make the turn.

Most recently the township removed the traffic system that photographed cars running red lights - it helped fill township coffers but accidents increased.

They changed the circle two or three times and recently made it an intersection with delayed traffic signals. It still has the highest accident incidence in Warren County.

"M" is for March or Mud

"M" is for March and for Mud. Today, people simply do not realize what happens when the weather warms and the frost goes out of the grounds and the good earth turns to mud. Up until the 1970's, there were still some dirt roads in the poorer townships but now even the tertiary roads are hard-surfaced as are most driveways and all mall parking lots. Throughout human history, footpaths, trails and roads turned to mud every spring and were virtually impassable. The wagon trains of the 1840s had to wait until the trails dried up before the settlers could start westward. Today people really don't know much about mud, but Teddy knew about mud even though he wasn't the sharpest knife in the drawer.

Teddy was a great big Polish bachelor farmer who survived by virtue of sheer strength and total stubbornness. The farm was not too neat and the house was kept barely livable by his aging auntie housekeeper. In his younger days, Teddy routinely carried two at a time full ten-gallon milk cans out of the milk house and hoisted them up onto a flatbed truck. Even in later years, he was still all muscle with wrists about the size of most people's ankles, due to his hand milking and mucking out the barn before and after school when he was a kid.

Now in his forties, Teddy had acquired a John Deere 60 with a #45 loader to move the manure piled outside the barn during the winter. He knew how important it was to spread the steaming stuff and get it plowed under to fertilize the crops. So, in the spring, he made repeated trips out of the barnyard, onto the county road with his manure spreader. Thus, mud and muck were dragged out onto the street.

At the time, it was customary to station recent graduates of the State Police Academy out in the rural counties to give them some experience. One new officers saw the mess on the pavement, turned on his red light and siren and followed Teddy and his John Deere. Teddy was only doing eight mph maximum and figured the officer was after a speeder so Teddy turned into the field and put the spreader in gear. When he looked back, he saw a police car stuck in the mud and splattered with cow poop. The officers radioed for reinforcements and by the time Teddy had the manure spread there were two more State Police blocking his gateway.

Teddy couldn't figure out what was going on but he decided he had better stop and find out when he saw the police with their guns drawn. As he got down off of the tractor, the officers tried to handcuff him but to no avail-his wrists were simply too large for the handcuffs to snap shut. Teddy kept yelling, 'What did I do???" as he shook the officers off. Things were rapidly deteriorating into a Rodney King scenario when the County Sheriff, who had heard the police call, arrived. The sheriff knew Teddy and was able to defuse the situation before someone got hurt. The sheriff explained to the officers that it was almost impossible to keep mud off of the road before a car skidded and had a wreck. They all agreed that the police would not put Teddy in jail if he would scrape the mud from the road and wash the police car. The resisting arrest charges still stood and as Teddy pondered the events of the day, he decided he had better call a local lawyer who had grown up on a nearby farm and who knew about both mud and Teddy.

"What the _ _ _ _?"

The Easton (PA) Circle has always been bad. Back in horse and buggy days the trolleys with their big overhang on each end would occasionally squash a buggy. Sixty years ago, my father-in-law was afraid of the Easton Circle although the similar Oxford Circle in Northeast Philadelphia did not bother him at all. Recent changes with traffic cones did not seem to help much and in my estimation made things worse. There has always been considerable traffic around the circle and the occasional fender bender. Fast forward to June 21, 2014 and any stranger (motorist) trying to figure out how to find Rte. 611 North would probably think, "What the _ _ _ _?" In addition to the usual traffic, there were dozens and dozens of antiques, foreign cars, hot rods and modifieds coming and going around the circle, then back and forth on Northampton Street - a Cruise Night with a different twist.

Perhaps a hundred special interest cars were parked in the quadrants around the circle, and the streets were full of people like it was Saturday nights in the 1950's. People eating and drinking at European style sidewalk tables, couples holding hands, an occasional couple dancing to the DJ's music. (Fred Antunes and his dancing partner) and Dave Schomp commenting on the pretty ladies wandering around.

I don't know if any real drag races took place on Northampton Street that evening as happened years ago. I recall once watching an old 1939 Buick Coupe beat a brand-new wheel-squealing 1950 Ford Convertible at every light on that (which was then) the main drag. I also recall getting a ticket for drag racing with my 1953 Oldsmobile, a visit to attorney Dimassi, a bottle of Seagram's 7 for the Easton policeman and my ticket disappearing "Pouf". Ah yes, I remember it well. Thanks to the city and DJ Jimmy for a different kind of "Cruise Night". See you on the next Cruise Night on the circle in Easton.

PS: Ask Vice President Joe Vasko about being in the back seat while cruising Northampton Street, oh so long ago.

What If?

It's been years since Henry Ford introduced his Model "T" car in 1908. It was very technologically advanced at the time and remained basically unchanged until the Model "A" came out in 1928. It has been estimated that there are perhaps a quarter of a million left (running, in pieces and stashed away in barns) of the twenty million built. You don't see too many on the roads today since the maximum cruising speed is 35-40 miles per hour and everybody drives 70-75 now. I stick to back roads with mine and have flashing red strobe lights on the back because I don't want to get rear-ended. How NASCAR drivers go 180 miles per hour only six inches apart is beyond me. They call it drafting and I call it nuts. The race cars are essentially identical today and are really only rolling billboards.

It's tempting to play "What if" with the NASCAR story. If the flat head Ford V8 guys had not kicked Bill France out of stock car racing on Daytona Beach, he would probably never have launched V8 NASCAR. His 1939 Buick Century coupe with factory dual carburetors, beat the pants off the Ford V8s and prompted rule changes. NASCAR race cars now are stock only in that they are stock right out of Jimmy Hendrick's racing garage in Charlotte, North Carolina.

I had a chance to visit his speed shop and racing museum and found out that NASCAR cars now differ mostly in the decals, now called wraps that represent grills, head lights and tail lights. Oh, for the good old days when Herb Thomas and Marshal Teague would get stock cars off the dealer's lot and race them, and back then when we rednecks put a Lincoln engine in a 37 Ford coupe and raced it ourselves like Jimmy Johnson. That was real stock car racing

TOMCATS

Some used to say, you can't beat Chevrolet
Which was abhorred, by friends of Ford.
Today we can't feel pride in a Tokyo mobile
And pound on our chest to say ours is best.
For it's just so plain and we're now too urbane.
I know it's absurd, but I have just heard
That back in the boonies, there are some loonies
Who are full grown men, with compulsive yen.
To bleed green, for a certain machine,
With others irrational for Case International.
But me, I have no pride, paint can be iron oxide.
The color of a tractor isn't a big factor.
Turned on I ain't by the smell of the paint.
Tractors come and go. In many various hues.
They come and go like tomcats do.
Whether big and small and any color at all.
Just give no trouble and it suits me just fine.
And a tractor will stay here like the feline.
My tractor colors are mixed, and like cats they get
fixed.
When I flicked a crumb from a donut
The auctioneer says, "Man, now you own it."
So like it or not, I use it a lot.
But good, better, or best I can't decide.
And to give me some semblance of pride

And put this matter for me once aside,
I just let our old tomcat decide.
So I planned a survey with graphs all so curvy
And I stayed well hidden, and watched this big kitten.
First he spritzed the Farmall tire real good.
Then jumped on the IH hood
To wet upon its exhaust pipe.
And that's why it smells so awful ripe.
Now I have this tremendous fear
He will wash down my John Deere.
And he climbed on the John Deere seat
To curl up in a ball, oh so neat.
He yawned and took a nice long rest.
I guess John Deere's are the best!

My dad and the 730

The Upper Class

Mark was only a couple of years out of Del Val College with an AG Science Degree when he got a job as working farm manager at the Duke Estate. It was quite common for the ultra-rich to have a country estate with formal gardens, greenhouses, a pretentious home and a dairy herd. The DuPonts had a purebred Holstein herd at Winterthur and so did Cyril Johnson of J&J near New Brunswick. Her pretty Jersey cattle were Doris Duke's pets and received the very best of care and feed: cost was no object. Doris Duke was the "poor little rich girl", sole heir to the tobacco fortune and Duke Industries. She was also eccentric[1] as only the rich and famous can afford to be. Very eccentric.

Doris had several homes in exotic places like the French Riviera and on Diamond Head on the big island of Hawaii. She would want a certain Rembrandt painting shipped the cheapest way to Hawaii, and would tell Mark to drop what he was doing and go out behind the barn and get old lumber off of the wood pile and build a crate for the painting and take it to Newark Airport and air freight it.

She had lots of friends in High Society and would go shopping with Imelda Marcos[2] for shoes at the Neiman Marcus store in New York City and then call Mark to pick up the purchases with the farm truck because she was too cheap to pay to have them delivered.

Malcolm Forbes Sr. was a neighbor and would occasionally drop by and visit with Doris. Then he started to come to see Mark. He would arrive on his BMW motorcycle wearing a tee shirt, shorts and flip flops and would bat the breeze with Mark as Mark finished up milking Doris's prized Jersey cows. Then as Mark washed up the milking machines, Malcolm would chase the cows out of the stable, scrape the cow flops into the manure gutter[3] and put hay in the mangers for the cows' breakfast. This from a multimillionaire who yearned for the good old redneck country life. After a beer (or two) while resting on a hay bale, they would take off on their motorcycles thru the woods on trails Mark had pushed out with Doris's bulldozer.[4] One evening when they were having a particularly good race, Malcolm just clipped a tree stump and broke the cylinder head off of the flat engine BMW. Malcolm escaped unhurt and got on the back of Mark's old Harley and they went back to the buildings, got Doris'

---

[1] She also had many husbands

[2] Imelda Marcos was the wife of President Marcos, dictator of the Philippines, and was reported to have 1000 pairs of shoes.

[3] "One thing I hope to live and see, I know how long twill be, till every cow gets out the door without pooping on the floor" Bob Frey 1972

[4] The Duke Estate consisted of perhaps one-thousand acres of woodland, farm fields, formal gardens, an arboretum and cow pastures, all surrounded by a six-foot high stone wall with sharp stones cemented on top.

The Upper Class (continued)

tractor and loader and put the BMW on the scrap pile. Needless to say, Malcolm got another motorcycle.

Mark was able to convince Doris that the farm (he) really needed a new grain harvesting combine, and so Doris called around to all the John Deere dealers to get the very best price. Doris struck a deal with the woman who was the brains at Piel Brothers (who incidentally always wore bib overalls, leather gloves and pink lipstick) in Pittstown. The big bright and shiny green machine was soon delivered to the Duke Estate and Mark could hardly wait to drive it.

It was early Fall and Mark decided it was time to harvest high moisture corn, so he started up the Model 4420 John Deere, turned on the air conditioner and radio and went out to the cornfield to shell corn. Being young and adventurous he kept pushing the variable speed lever ahead until he plugged up the machine all the way from the corn head, the feeder house, the cylinders, the beater drum, the sieves, the fan to the straw walkers. Plugged it up solid and burned off the main vee belts, trying to unplug it.

Mark went back to the mansion house and told Doris (who was known to have a violent temper and a vast vocabulary of cuss words) that the brand-new combine was plugged up. He did carefully not say, "I plugged up the new combine."

Doris said not a word but slammed the door in a huff and the next morning, after consulting her latest copy of "Who's Who in America" she made a 6 am person to person (Eastern time) call to John Deere CEO, Mr. Hewitt, in Waterloo, Iowa. Doris proceeded to tell him that his combines were no ____ing good. Blurry-eyed from being awakened, Mr. Hewitt stammered, "Who is this?" Doris responded that she was the largest landowner in the state of New Jersey and she was going to purchase his ___ ___ Company and the first thing she was going to do was fire Mr. Hewitt. Needless to say, she got another new combine and Mark was very, very careful with it.

True story as related by Mark.

CLIP-CLOP

The clip-clop of the milkman's horse was a common early morning sound in urban areas through the World War II period. After this automobile ownership became more common and supermarkets appeared. Mr. Snyder made a good, although hard, living with his delivery route. Year round, summer and winter, good weather or bad, he loaded his enclosed wagon with heavy wooden cases of glass milk bottles at a local creamery. One was located one hundred yards east of Shimer School. It was operated by Mr. Kearns and has been converted to a home. Every PM, local farmers would deliver fresh, warm milk to the creamery in ten-gallon, eighty-pound tinned steel milk cans. The creamery operator would then pasteurize the milk and bottle it in steam-sterilized heavy glass bottles imprinted with either the creamery name or the name of the delivery man.

Mr. Snyder, who was known as "Wingy" (probably a corruption of Wayne) would then proceed with his loaded wagon west on South Main to the ice plant located across the street from Pursel's mill. The ice-producing machinery used a Freon- free refrigerant-ammonia. He purchased ice blocks, chipped them with an ice pick and iced down the milk bottles. His route covered Huntington, Parkside, Shimer Manor and Alpha Borough. Like the city postman today, Mr. Snyder had to go up on every porch, leave the full bottles and retrieve the empties. His horse knew precisely where to stop which was amazing since the horse was blind. "Moon" blindness is a somewhat rare malady affecting horses which causes progressive blindness. Man and horse were inseparable after years of working together. The man providing the food and shelter and in return the horse assisting the man. Simple and total symbiosis.

It had been rainy for a week and Mr. Snyder unhitched, stabled, fed, watered and rubbed down his horse before going home himself. Beginning around 8 pm on July 10, 1945 a violent storm dropped 6 inches of rain on the Lopatcong Watershed which drains the north slope of the Montana Mountain (aka Scott's Mountain) and a large portion of Lopatcong, Greenwich, Harmony, and Pohatcong Townships. The cloud burst could not be absorbed by the saturated soil, and all the water rushed down the tiny trout stream which separated Phillipsburg and Pohatcong Township. The Lopatcong Creek flooded South Main Street and Mr. Snyder's horse barn which still stands today on the north side of South Main Street in the 1300 block opposite the tombstone display.

The next morning Mr. Snyder found the water subsiding, his barn and milk wagon intact but his work-mate, confidant and pet were gone. He definitely remembered tying the horse up the night before with the night halter. He asked around South Main Street thinking somebody might have untied the horse as the waters rose. Nobody was of any help. He searched all forenoon and spent the afternoon calling his customers

(Continued on next page)

CLIP-CLOP (continued)

explaining his predicament and apologizing because he could not make his deliveries. He spent a sleepless night worrying about what to do. Upgrading to a motor truck was out of the question since no new vehicles were being manufactured for civilian use, and good used trucks were really scarce. He was devastated and his very livelihood was in jeopardy.

The flood waters went down rapidly but left a stinking muddy mess as does any flood. The July 10, 1945 cloudburst had set water rushing down the Lopatcong creek washing out septic tanks, cesspools and outhouses. All of this was deposited downstream and was recognized as a health hazard that had to be cleaned up. Fortunately, unaffected people in the neighborhood pitched in and helped.

The flooding was made worse on the east end of Phillipsburg's South Main Street because at an earlier time, Pursel's Agway Grist Mill had been powered by a water wheel and the dam and feed race still existed blocking the flood waters.[1] At this time Pursel's Mill bought, processed and stored large amounts of grain for animal feed and this all got soaked and soon started to stink and to spoil, Pursel also owned three Mack Trucks and the rushing flood washed away the garage and upset those big trucks into the stream bed.[2]

Meanwhile, poor ole' Mr. Snyder was still missing his horse. Then he heard a rumor that there was a horse on the island in the middle of the Delaware River.[3]

He grabbed a rope halter, found somebody with a row boat and set out for the island. His horse was standing directly among the weeds, mud and storm toppled trees on a high point of the island. The blind horse responded immediately to his master's voice and with some difficulty "Wingy" got the horse to swim back to shore. Home at last in its own stall with a manger full of fresh hay and a little oats, the horse got a good rub down and "Wingy" was delighted to have his coworker, confidant and pet back with him and I bet the horse was pretty happy, too.

[1] The mill pond was at one time part of the Morris Canal and the flood waters followed the abandoned canal bed which added to the disaster.

[2] The Pursels immediately started cleaning up their property and eventually put their Mack Trucks back in service. Two employees (Sam Herring and Floyd Apgar) completely disassembled the trucks and washed off every single bearing and gear of the engines, transmissions and differentials.

[3] The island is visible to the south of the Route 78 Bridge over the Delaware.

Smokey

As you flip the auto parts store calendar over to May, you realize that there is yet another painting of an old garage surrounded by a couple of dozen old junk cars, and you might wonder if such places really exist.

At last count "Smokey" had at least that many clunkers including a 1949 Frazer, a 1936 Plymouth, a 1937 Chevy Coupe, a 1938 Chevy Sedan and a 1946 Chevy ½ ton pick-up mixed in with lawn mowers, ski mobiles, ATV's, snow blowers, leaf blowers, chain saws and outboard motors. There were tires, wheels, springs, axles and engines in, around and under a box trailer. A rollback and a forklift stood ready for emergencies.

The work bay has a work bench, a hydraulic lift, torch and welder right out of the 1950's, dating from when his father operated a Sinclair station there. (Remember the green dinosaur signs?) The office sports an ancient Coca Cola cooler, a television, a microwave and two old reclining barber chairs upholstered with old carpet, deer hide and duct tape. (The original LA-Z-BOY). On the wall there are gun racks, fishing poles, deer antlers and a mounted jackalope head. (Did they really ever exist?) The walls are covered with "stuff" piled up from the floor almost to the ceiling.

Excuse me, dear reader, for I ramble here, so returning back outside at "Smokey's" we find an ancient glass front refrigerated cooler. During the summer, he sells produce and people come for miles around thinking he grows the early sweet corn and tomatoes. The vegetables may very well come from Philadelphia's Dock St. or Haddonfield Farmers' Market, but nobody seems to know or care. It must be the ambiance.

This is definitely not a Mr. Goodwrench Franchise, although Smokey is clever at fixing things. Turnaround time is anywhere from fifteen minutes to a couple of weeks to never. One never knows. You may find him outside lying under a car with his feet sticking out from underneath or asleep in a barber chair or flipping venison steaks on a charcoal grill with his welder's gloves. So if you need something fixed, don't say I sent you.

Note to reader: Remember that the above story is fiction and has no resemblance or relation to any persons living or dead and that you did not hear it from me.

* * * * * * *

HAIR TODAY – GONE TOMORROW

There was a man from Cape May

Who bought himself a toupee

As bad as George Will's

And he'd have it still

If it hadn't blown away

Schultzy the Barrel Man

It is a nice dwelling with exposed beams. Originally it had been a typical Pennsylvania Dutch Barn with a ramp to the haymow and an overshot protecting the stable downstairs so that the winter sun would warm the cow stalls. The haymows had once been full of sweet-smelling hay for the animals. In the 1870's the Lehigh Valley and the Jersey Central Railroads had cut through the farm just behind the barn, and the fields were eventually sold off for development.

Main Street was known as "Dish Water Alley". It was a commonly accepted fact that if you left your car windows open, some housewife would throw slops at your car. Eventually the town decided to build a badly needed sewer plant in the meadow. The cows were sold and "Schultzy" decided to go into another business.

He made high racks extending out over the cab of his one-ton Chevy truck, and he was in business with probably only minimal insurance, certainly no commercial driver license or HAZMAT license. He got the idea from "Dusty" the Bag Man who made his rounds of farms and bought used empty feed bags, sorted them, and resold them back to the original feed mills. Schultzy dealt in barrels.

All service stations at one time got motor oil in bulk, and all industries shipped their products in fifty-five-gallon drums. These sat around empty until Schultzy made his rounds and took them off their hands.

Schultzy would rinse out the barrels of whatever evil contents they contained, store them in his barn, and when he had a truckload from one particular company he would return them to the source and get paid.

It was rumored that his run-down house was full of expensive antiques and that he was the richest man in town, except for the undertaker and that is another story. And today (2017) that old barn is now a private home. I really would not even want my dog to live there because of what Schultzy dumped.

* * * * * * *

Sandy Hager's painting of the old mill and bridge in Finesville, NJ

Model T Ford Sausage

1 model T Ford car 1909-1927

1 manifold cooker installed on right side of engine

2 lb. sweet sausage

3 tbsp of Cabela's Hunting Season Rub.

1 can of spaghetti sauce

1 large onion

1 large pepper

Parmesan cheese

Hoagie rolls

Tin foil to line cooker

Slice sausage into 6-inch length, long ways

Dice onion and pepper

Sprinkle with Cabella's Rub

Place in manifold cooker

Pour in spaghetti sauce

Cover with tin foil

Retard spark on Ford, set throttle to ¼

Set parking brake, crank until engine starts

Invite 3 or 4 people to get in

Drive 40 miles on secondary roads

Enjoy scenery, sounds and smells

Find a shade tree in cow pasture

Serve sausage on hoagie rolls

Top with Parmesan cheese

Sit on running board and enjoy life!

PS: Model T Ford's exhaust manifolds get red hot.

Lures, Rods and Reels

Sometimes I wonder what got people interested in their hobbies, and I've come to the conclusion it usually starts early in life. If you want a cat to be a "mouser" somebody (mother cat or owner) has to give it a taste of fresh and preferably bloody mouse meat early in life; otherwise the kitten will probably grow up to a life of naps, cat food, filling litter boxes and scratching furniture.

I know some avid hunters whose families started them hunting at an early age triggered by mankind's primeval urge for protein. I have a good friend who lives and breathes hunting. He was raised on a neighboring farm with a half-dozen siblings, and when he was six years old his father first took him hunting. His father would hook up the little Ford 8 N farm tractor to the flat bed hay wagon and they would set off with shot gun and flashlight to hunt "Night Rabbits". His father would let Louie drive with the small gray tractor idling in first gear. (Today six-year-olds drive baby Jeeps with no problem). Since the driver straddled the tractor frame, it was easy to push down on both the clutch and brake. Louie's dad would scramble out over the differential and the Ferguson three-point hitch on to the wagon tongue with the 12-gauge. He would then stand up on the wagon like George Washington crossing the Delaware. Then it was "Bang Bang," provender with meat on the table. When Louie was nine he got a small 410 shot gun, his turns on the wagon, and his destiny to be a hunter.

I also know a guy who is an avid fly fisherman. He can talk for hours about making lures, various rods and reels, the nuances of ripples and riffles, the rocks and sandbars, the twists and turns, the macroinvertebrates and the fishing holes in trout streams all over the country. His father took him and his older brother fishing when he was four years old. He still remembers catching his very first fish. From then on he was hooked on fishing. (Bad Pun). Only recently did he learn that his brother had somehow stuck that fish on his hook when he wasn't looking and threw it in unbeknownst to him. He wished they had never told him. Ignorance is bliss.

I guess I got interested in antique vehicles with my Grandfather Hance's 1920 Star car with its glass flower vases. I used to play in Grandpa Frey's 1929 Chevrolet with its wooden steering wheel and bright green disc wheels and especially enjoyed riding in Uncle John's 1924 International stake body truck. It was a neat old truck and I go to the Macungie Pennsylvania Truck Show every Father's Day hoping to find one like it.

1939

Hemmings Retro and Bennington, Vermont

We pulled off of the interstate on to the main street of the town looking for gasoline, (the whole world is looking for gasoline). We pulled up to the pump. We noted it was blue and yellow - Sunoco. We wondered if Sunoco (Sun Oil Company) was still in business; if it was a wholly owned subsidiary of some multinational corporation; or if it might be a candidate for a hostile take-over by the Chinese.

The attendant came to the car window and I told him to fill'er up before the price went up. He stuck the nozzle into the EPA approved Bung Hole, which I understand recaptures the fumes and puts them back in the underground tank. Where they go from there I don't know. You will have to ask region member John G. who is our expert on petroleum and who does not (as of yet) wear a turban and drive a camel.

Then I noted that the attendant was busily washing the windshield. Actually, there were two attendants and the other was cleaning the back window and the taillights. This can't be Pennsylvania and it can't be 2005 A.D. Real disbelief set in when one of them asked if I wanted the oil checked. Just imagine. Was it some kind of time warp?

NO. It was summer 2005 in Bennington, Vermont at Hemming's Retro (not Repro) 1930's Gas Station decorated with brilliant blue and yellow. I paid the guy and parked the car so we could use the potty, which turned out to be right out of the 1930's. Enough said. One thing Hemmings did was to fill in the old grease pit. A black hole indeed.

Remember when the 1938 Buick's had 32 grease fittings? (Incidentally John G.'s trademark logo is copyrighted*). Every one of those fittings had to be greased every one-thousand miles. Back then the mechanic went down a slippery set of steps into a long narrow pit and someone drove the car in, straddling the hole, so that the grease monkey could reach all those "zerk" fittings.

Back to the twenty first century and Hemmings remodeling. Almost every square inch of what was the station's Garage Bay Area is now covered with memorabilia Repro signs, books and toy model cars of every description (Even more than our treasurer Jerry Kearns has- if you can believe it). All this stuff is for sale and of course Hemmings is in business to make money. Their corporate headquarters is just up the street and Hemmings is a major employer in Bennington. Antique cars have been good for Hemmings and Hemmings has been good for the collector hobby. It's sort of like Charlie Wilson once saying, "What's Good For General Motors Is Good For The USA." But now that I think about it, Charlie Wilson's statement may work conversely since General Motors stock is down to $36.58 as GM posted a $318,000,000.00 loss in the first quarter of 2005.

PS: Hemmings publishes a monthly 200-page book of automotive trivia and advertisements.

John G. had a gas station on Easton, PA Rte. 248 and owned a 1938 Buick which he had an artist draw a picture of that he copyrighted and then used as his own logo.

Freyr Ivan Dorothy Midget

Last fall while my wife and I were on vacation, our son Rob took my 1951 Chevy pick-up and had my name painted on the doors. He also had the rear bumper painted with a picture of my "Midget" cow.

I found this tiny premature calf in the manure gutter one winter morning in early 1970. I sloshed some warm water on it and dragged it around front to the manger so its mother could lick it off and clean it up. It survived, was named "Freyr Ivan Dorothy Midget", grew up to weigh 1600 pounds and became a bit of a pet.* During her lifetime she gave over 200,000 pounds (pints) of milk, was considered a gold medal dam and was classified "excellent" by the Holstein Friesian Association of America.

Classification is a process similar to AACA judging, and it involves trained personnel evaluating purebred animals according to standards adopted by the Breed Association as to what the perfect ideal true type Holstein Friesian Cow should look like. (The Classifiers come out to farms).

Having an "excellent" Gold Medal Dam is like having a National AACA First Prize Car. The average schmuck like me stands very little chance since those dairymen with money can afford both better (read expensive) breeding stock and bull semen. Thus, it is similar to when big bucks help get trophies for the trailer queens.

We actually had a 20th birthday party for our "Midget" cow and invited the neighboring farmers. The following summer we had to euthanize her (lethal injection) and we gave her a decent burial. No hamburger here - she was special. Now every time I look at my not particularly special truck I can ruminate (bad pun) about my very special, long gone big pet.

*The cattle breed associations have an identification system similar to the American Kennel Club in which the first name is the Breeder's prefix (in my case it is "Freyr", the Scandinavian God of Agriculture). The second name is the bull's name (sire of the animal). The third name is the dam (mother) and the last name is its proper name. Since a Holstein's black and white spots stay the same throughout its lifetime the animal can thus be identified and registered in the Breed Herd Book. A purebred cow's ancestry can thus be traced back to foundation stock imported from the Netherlands over 125 years ago, and that's a whole lot better than most of us can do with our own family tree.

Independence Day Parade-Best of Show

I had just finished reading last month's Body Squeaks with Vangie Schweitzer's interview of Hank Freyer and his plans to participate in the Lebanon, N.J. Independence Day Parade when the Beckers called to see if I wanted to go to it. Frank and Trish came from that area originally and have friends there. I had heard about that big parade but had never attended. It includes marching bands, patriotic floats, and fire and emergency squads and has been held for 100 years. It is famous like Mummers Day and the Kentucky Derby.

So my daughter-in-law and youngest grandson followed the Beckers and their teenage daughter and were parked in a shady cul-de-sac. Sure enough, Hank was there with his family and we had a very nice visit. They brought both his Model T and Model A Ford open cars. There were some nice cars including a black 1949 Ford sedan and a 1972 Vega station wagon with a sign that said, "If you remember Vegas, you are an Antique!" There was a 1968 Chevy like I once owned and a pretty bright orange Allis Chalmers tractor pulling a hay wagon. Several green and yellow John Deere "putt putts" also waited for the parade to start.

Our end of the parade got going an hour late and proceeded through Main Street with its brightly painted Victorian Houses and flower gardens. Pure Americana right out of the "Music Man" movie. Hundreds of people were relaxing on sidewalks and front porches enjoying the parade.

When we got to the judge's stand, a lady stepped out with a two-foot high gold trophy and they announced that Becker's 1951 Chevy pick-up had won "Best of Show". It was as if Frank had it all planned by bringing his wife and daughter along. A couple of hundred yards further and up a steep hill the Beckers' truck stopped and would not start. The balance of the parade was stopped in its tracks. Amazingly eight or nine men immediately appeared from front porches and sidewalks and pushed the award-winning truck to the top of the hill and out of the street so the parade could continue. Somebody produced a can of lawn mower gas and the truck coughed to life. They managed to get home ok. And like "Paul Harvey's The Rest of The Story" - is that four days later the engine on Frank's Beechcraft airplane stalled while flying into Lancaster Airport. He had to ditch it in a cornfield. The plane was wrecked, but Frank is ok.

Ford Motor Company's 75th Anniversary

In 1978, we trailered the Model T Ford out to Dearborn for the Ford Motor Company's 75th anniversary. It was its second trip there. In 1953 Bernie Hawk drove it from the Lehigh Valley to Ford's 50th and decided to sell it when he got back. While there we were given a tour of the Ford Car Factory and recently had a chance to again see how cars were built today. What a change.

I had the opportunity to visit the Smyrna, Tennessee Nissan Automobile Factory where they turn out two-thousand vehicles a day in a highly automated process. Body panels are stamped out of steel that arrives in rolls by truck. In the case of Nissan's Xterra, the whole side panel is one stamping from the cowl line all the way back to the tail light buckets, including rocker panel door jams all the way up to about three inches above the door openings.

SUV's still have a frame which is purchased from an outside supplier and delivered just in time for the preprogrammed robots to add floor pan, side panels, cowl and roof panels which are tack welded together by robots. The welds are not continuous as that would warp the stampings. The joints are then filled in with goo like liquid nails which seals the body. Cars had rain gutters thirty years ago but today the seam where roof joins side panels is supposed to keep rain water off of your seat when you get in. The assembly line moves each vehicle through a water detergent bath then it is blown dry and given a coat of primer with a minus electrical charge. Subsequent paint has a positive charge. Robots spray paint into every conceivable part. The paint is water based and the over-spray is collected in a trough of water under the paint line and re-used. Engines and transmissions arrive from Dechero, Tennessee just in time to be installed. Dash assemblies, doors, fenders and hoods are put on by robots as the line moves. Humans do assist at these stations but do little or no lifting. The proper color seats and floor mats come in at just the right time by computer controlled robots. The Smyrna plants has one-thousand robots, most of which are in the body assembly plant.

There are about four-thousand employees working two shifts, thirty-seven hours a week starting at $16.00 per hour moving up to $25.00. When demand requires it they work 60 hours per week. This is excellent pay in the mid-south. It is a nonunion shop. They have no layoffs.

General Motors built a Saturn Plant* nearby but the United Automobile Workers Union threatened to shut down all of GM facilities if Saturn wasn't a union plant. Wages are similar but when demand is slack Saturn lays its people off. Also, Nissan has only four-hundred retirees, so the pension cost per vehicle is negligible.

My observation is that Nissan vehicles are very efficiently and well-built today and are a far cry from Nissan Company's Datsun Vehicles that appeared on our shores in 1958.

*Saturn's are no longer made.

English...1-2-3

Donald asked his former English teacher if she remembered him. Her response was that she was sorry she did not because she had had so many pupils over the years. Donald was disappointed because he was certain she would remember him. After all, it was he to whom she once said, "I simply cannot understand how your sister can be so brilliant and you are so stupid!"

Donald had taken high school freshman English for three years, and he sat in the very same seat in the right rear corner of the classroom right next to the radiator every one of those years.

Donald was not that stupid - in fact, he conceived a brilliant plan all on his own. He would enter the classroom, go to his seat and turn off the valve on the heat radiator. By the time the teacher was well into the day's lesson plan, the pipes would start banging and the teacher would say, "Donald, go find the janitor and tell him that there is something wrong with the heating system." Donald would blithely wander the halls for a while and eventually return to the English classroom. Once seated, he would open the valve when the teacher's back was turned. He would then concentrate on whether the pipes would stop banging before the closing bell rang.

There was a kid in high school,
Whom the English teacher did ridicule,
He suffered humiliation,
Never learned conjugation,
But the teacher he managed to fool.

PS: Donald is a member of the Lehigh Valley Region and with his wife attends our banquets, picnics, and occasionally cruise nights. He ran a highly successful electrical contracting business.

Chicken Buses, Mack Trucks and Memories

My wife and I took a Caribbean Cruise in late January 2014.[1] Mexico is certainly poor - no wonder the young men head north. Streets are narrow, no stop lights, speed bumps at every intersection. Houses with rebar sticking up so they can build an additional floor later on when they can afford it.[2] Mexican gasoline prices are fixed but uniformed attendants wash wind shields, check under the hood and put air in car tires.[3] Buses appear to be old American school buses painted in bright primary colors with gold leaf and murals decorating the sides. They now sport chrome grills, chrome stacks and shiny aluminum wheels. They are called "chicken buses" because it is universally common when visiting city cousins to bring a gift, and what could be more appropriate than a nice fat chicken?[4]

Costa Rica appears more prosperous with lots of trucks hauling containers. They do have traffic lights. We were on a farm tour and our guide pointed out coffee, sugar cane, melon, orchid farms and at one point said, "That's a truck farm" It was a truck junk yard filled with trucks and truck parts. It finally dawned on me that there were a lot of older Mack Trucks on the road there. They were the ones with the lopsided cabs and seldom seen in the states nowadays.[5] Someone must have bought these heavy haulers, shipped them to Costa Rico to be restored, rebuilt and reused.

The Panama Canal was the high point of the trip[6] for me. There was less than six inches of clearance on each side of the ship as it passed through the locks. It is amazing that the canal was built[7] over one-hundred years ago and has operated ever since. A new canal is under construction to allow even larger ships to pass. However, all work is currently at a standstill due to a conflict with the Spanish contractor and the Chinese financiers over cost overruns. It was a great trip. We highly recommend it, but don't wait until you are in your eighties like we did!

---

[1] No, we did not get sick

[2] I have known of instances here in the states when a young couple would build the basement, cover the floor boards with a canvas, and live in it until they could afford their home. But no more - now we have Planning Boards, Land Use Boards, Boards of Adjustments and most importantly lawyers. And so it goes.

[3] Hemmings Sonoco in Bennington, Vermont is the only place I know of that does it in America. In New Jersey it is mandatory that 10-year-old buses be retired.

[4] Reminds me of the tale of my Great-Grandmother "Charlotte" taking a crock of pot cheese on the Quakertown Trolley 110 years ago.

[5] Built right here in the Lehigh Valley and Dave Schomp may still have some.

[6] No pun intended, the canal actually passes over the Continental Divide.

[7] Using Lehigh Valley cement and no computer

Ford Celebrated its Centennial
with Brand New 1914 Model T Cars

In a hush-hush project started in late 1999, Ford restarted its Model T assembly line, building brand-new, 1914-version Touring Cars from scratch. The new models, based on the first mass-production versions of the "Car of the Century," are completely drivable. The mechanicals are true to the originals, and the five-passenger models offer the same four-cylinder power and two-speed transmissions that were standard on Model Ts of yesteryear. Styling, both inside and out, is also true to the original, from the brass headlights down to the huge 30-in. spoked wheels and ribbed running boards.

But don't bother trying because, no, you can't buy one.

Happy 100.

Ford Co. called on traditional and nontraditional suppliers to get the project under way. In all, six cars will be produced, each of top-grade quality. Each will bear a serial number starting with 2003001.

Once the decision was made, a small group of company engineers/enthusiasts gathered at an out-of-the-way machine shop near Detroit. The project posed major questions. Could new parts be available? Who would assemble the engines and transmissions? What about the timetables? In all, about 700 major parts had to be accounted for. Ford's managers found that many of their problems were solved by simply ordering from a catalog.

"We picked up 550 major parts from catalogs like Lang's Old Car Parts Company," reports Bill Leland, project manager. "But we also went to a couple of overseas suppliers to manufacture new parts. We got engine cranks from New Zealand and the wooden body frame from Sweden." In one odd engineering twist, an original engine block was sent to an Air Force laboratory in Ogden, Utah, for a CAT (computerized axial tomography) scan. That's right, the laboratory took a high-tech look inside the casting.

"We had some original prints of the engine casting," says Leland. "They showed us the same things we already knew about the outside of the engine. But we didn't know the shape of internal passages. Those CAT scan pictures sliced the block into thin layers, showed us exactly what we needed about forming the innards."

Also working in Leland's favor was the existence of many of the original 1914 models. "Over 200,000 came off the assembly lines that year, and there are a significant number still in collectors' hands. That creates a large demand for replacement parts and we benefited from that."

Under the hood is a 2.9-liter (176 cu.-in.) L-head four-cylinder engine. It is unadorned—no pumps, no injectors, no emissions equipment. Its 4.0:1 compression ratio is startlingly low—less than half that of a modern car. Output is weak too: 22.5hp and a red line of 1600 rpm. However, strong torque allows the engine to chug along at idle in high gear without noticeable strain. Top speed is 45 mph. A clutch and shifting system that includes the use of a long-throw handbrake allows the driver two forward and one reverse gears.

Getting behind the wheel can be both fun and daunting. Engine controls are left- and right-side levers attached to the steering column. The left one sets spark advance/retard while the right is the fuel feed. At the driver's feet are three pedals: the clutch/shifter, reverse and brake. At the left side of the driver's seat is the handbrake that does double duty as the transmission's Neutral position.

Proceeding in High gear you get to appreciate the genius of these vehicles. The most surprising things are its low noise and smooth ride. The engine, especially in High gear at moderate speed, produces little more than a hum as it perks along. And the ride, on the car's transverse leaf-spring suspension, is not as bumpy as you might expect. On Detroit city streets, it's as smooth as some of today's small sedans. But be careful of the steering. It is quick and the wheel reacts strongly to bumps and ruts.

Braking is a lot different from modern cars, though the results are similar if you mind your speed. The footbrake squeezes only the transmission. The handbrake leads directly to drum-type brakes at the rear wheels. In both cases, the rear wheels provide all the stopping power. That's fine if you don't exceed 30 to 35 mph.

One of the unique features of the vehicle is its lack of a pump of any kind, not even a fuel pump. That's why Model T drivers sometimes had to go uphill in Reverse when the gas tank was nearing empty. The idea is to have the gas drain down from its mid-chassis location by gravity when low on gas.

Ain't That A Kick?

However, Leland reassured us, "Just follow directions and it'll be fine. It takes a little time, but nothing will go wrong." Directions, it turns out, make up the complicated part. But knowing what is at stake, most folks follow them faithfully.

Here is the basic procedure: Lift up on the right side of hood and turn on the gas spigot (coming from the tank). Reach into the cockpit and retard the spark by pushing up on the left lever (this step is important). Set the gas lever by pushing down on the right lever a half-inch. Set the handbrake. Turn the brass knob on the right side of the instrument panel a quarter turn clockwise (rich mixture). Push in the crank until it connects with engine. Give it a yank to make sure it turns.

Now, pull out the choke wire twice to prime the engine while cranking. Go back inside and turn the ignition switch from off to "Battery." Go back around to the front, pull up on the crank handle clockwise one, two or three times. Yes! It starts. Not with a loud noise and shake, but a low, sure putt-putt. Finally, go back inside and advance the spark by turning the lever about 1 inch down, switch the ignition from "Battery" to "Magneto" and rest for about 5 minutes while the engine warms up. Return the choke to normal setting when the engine is running smoothly. And away we go.

The assembly shop has turned out six complete models. Ford will donate all six to as-yet-unnamed museums for permanent display. These twenty-first century 1914 reproes are in daily use in Ford's Dearborn Village.

SPECIFICATIONS: 2003 FORD MODEL T TOURING CAR	
ENGINE	2.9-liter inline four-cylinder
HORSEPOWER	22.5
REDLINE	1600 rpm
COMPRESSION RATIO	4.0:1
TRANSMISSION	two-speed manual
TOP SPEED	55 mph
LENGTH	148 in.
WHEELBASE	100 in.
HEIGHT	89 in.
WEIGHT	1200 pounds
TIRES	30 in. dia.
BRAKES	Rear only, footbrake to transmission, handbrake to rear wheels.

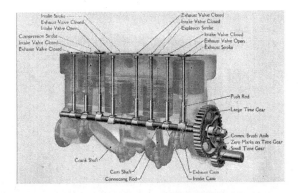

(See page ____)

Musicals

The Broadway play *Fiddler on the Roof* has a song in it called "Tradition". Traditions are important and are tied into nice memories, fun times, good friends and GREAT FOOD. I am afraid our local Region is in danger of losing its "Traditions".

I read with interest that this club is no longer going to have picnics. We no longer have spring and fall Banquets (Williams, The Palace, Hartman's, and Nazareth and Mt. Bethel Churches), do not have the Annual Springtown Show (admittedly a lot of work) and our fall tour to Hershey in October is to be casual with no attempt to stay together as a group to assist one another if need be. Of course, I'm willing to bet that more than half of those attending that Museum event will be driving late model cars. The show tune, "A Fine Romance This Is" is appropriate here – a fine old Car Club this is!

There is another old Broadway tune "Not While I'm Around" from the play *Sweeney Todd*.[1] There will be a picnic as long as I am around, at least in 2017, complete with a hay ride at Frey's Farm. Our Model T Ford was built in June 1917 (#1922575) and will be 100 then and we will have a party, a celebration. "Remember the song "Celebration"? A Tradition[2] nonetheless. So, you all (y'all) are invited. Traditions – Traditions. "Ah yes, I remember it well" as sung by Maurice Chevalier back in the 1960's.

[1] The *Sweeney Todd* play is based on an allegedly true story about a London barber who slit his clients' throats and his lady friend who made "the very best meat pies."

[2] Trudy and I have had a lot of untraditional fun with the Ford over the last 60 years we owned it. It has just been re-engined for its birthday.

Ford 100th Anniversary

It was really the best kept secret of the year 2003. If you belonged to the right car club you knew about it (Model T, Mustang, Thunderbird, etc.) and of course all the information was available on the Internet. As it was, over 90,000 people showed up over the five-day event, and the $24.00 ticket was good for any and all days. Had Ford really advertised this, its 100th Anniversary, it would have been like another World's Fair. Anybody remember 1940 and 1964 in New York?

Even with the Hertz satellite guidance system on the rented Taurus, we could not find our designated blue field parking area (Was it really back at Hershey?) so we parked across busy Dearborn Avenue in the Henry Ford Library Parking Lot. As we hiked the third of a mile to the entrance we caught a glimpse through chain-link fencing of the monster trucks, the professional bull rider bulls, the 100-foot-high Ford Blue Centennial Structure and of course the majestic "glass house corporate center."

We queued up along with a couple of thousand others and had our "passports" processed by the events management people Ford had contracted with to run the show, and run the show well they certainly did. The food was good and reasonably priced, the lines were short, and the toilets were air-conditioned.

The sun came out shortly after we landed in Detroit, but it was fully as muddy in Dearborn on the landscaped corporate grounds as it was back home in our cow pasture. Rows and rows of antique Lincoln show cars had been assigned a particularly squishy area and were not nearly as well detailed as they had been when they pulled onto the once manicured grounds. In an attempt to solve the mud problem, event management people were bringing in pine bark wood chips by the Michigan centipede truckloads. A Michigan centipede is a huge low wheel dump truck with at least three more dead axles spaced under the frame. How they negotiate sharp turns is beyond this writer.

Hundreds of restored T-Birds, Mustangs, Model A's and B's were on display all classified as number two or better. At least a couple hundred model T's showed up including a dozen and a half that were <u>DRIVEN</u> in from California the previous week, with two of them coming from New Zealand. Needless to say, all of these had Warford transmissions or Ruxtel rears and also needless to say all had Rocky Mountain Brakes. Ford had one vehicle from every year of its production parked right in front of the corporate headquarters along with outstanding vehicles representative of its foreign subsidiaries. They even had the famous Red Volvo P 1800 Coupe with 2,000,000 miles on it and it looked like new, today in 2017 it has 3,000,000 miles. Yes, dear reader, Ford bought Volvo reputedly to get the elaborate crash test facilities Volvo had developed in Sweden. And of course, there were lots and lots of rods and modifieds parked in their own special area.

Each Ford division had its own air-conditioned tent measuring perhaps 100 by 300 feet with carpets and cleaning ladies vacuuming up the mud we tracked in. The latest models were on display and you were allowed to sit in them to your heart's content and no salesmen came to pester you. My son was happy as a clam to have his photo taken in the James Bond XK convertible with the mounted rocket guns. In addition, each marquee had its own far out concept cars on display but no one was allowed to sit in them. Darn it!!

There was one tent devoted entirely to important Ford racecars and another with Ford approved after-market vendors of reproduction and speed equipment parts. Motorola, a Ford subsidiary, had a tent honoring 100 years of aviation. Here they had flight simulators and I was able to successfully fly a DC-3 over Alaskan mountains. Ford/Motorola had put a lot of money into the reproduction of the Wright Brothers' Flyer and developed a flight simulator for that. Behind this tent a couple of men who built the exact replica of Wilbur and Orville's own homemade engine and were trying to get theirs to run. It popped, snorted and backfired like a two-cylinder John Deere tractor with a wet magneto. It's a wonder that the Wright Brothers' plane ever flew at all.

Ford had air-conditioned buses waiting to take visitors to the new environmental and OSHA friendly pickup truck factory where the assembly line moves up and down so workers don't have to stretch or stoop. Buses then took us to Ford's test track facility where we got to drive the new and supposedly un-up settable Volvo SUV's around and through traffic cones set up on the track. Parked here also was a nice old Ford Tri-Motor Plane and a tiny three-cylinder monoplane that old Henry had at one point considered mass producing. It was look and don't touch but sheer happiness for me!

Back on the grounds of the corporate center volunteers put on a show in which they assembled a Model T in less than five minutes and if you were willing to wait in line you could get a free ride in an original Model T as it wound a track with displays showing highlights of Ford production through the decades. These Model T's were supplied and driven by dozens of owners who volunteered. Lots of credit must be given to these fine folks and to Mr. Bill Barth who set this up. Antique car people are nice people indeed.

The professional Bull Riders put on shows and the best part is never shown on TV. It is when the bulls simply refuse to go back in the chute and go after the clowns. And believe it or not, I actually petted one of the bulls. Three guys on motorcycles entertained by going all directions around and around in a 25-foot strap iron sphere. And not to be forgotten were the monster truck shows. They were all Fords and were jeep-leaping old Chevrolet Monte Carlos which all were painted (you guessed it) Fomco Blue. The squashed Chevy's were towed away and replacements immediately pulled into place. If ever there was an event to gladden the hearts of Ford fans, it was this – the car event of the century and with no hard sell whatsoever.

A Good Year

I made up my mind that I was going to all the car shows I possibly could in 2003. After milking cows for over 50 years, I figured I deserved that luxury and because it was 100 years since the Ford Motor Company was founded. 1903 really must have been a great year with International Harvester, Crayola, Harley Davidson and the Wright Bros. companies all getting off the ground. (Poor pun) Also both my parents were born in 1903.

Our Lehigh Valley AACA Region Tour on April 27th was a success with stops at the Kutztown Plow Boys Festival and the Reading Airplane Museum. Our club was badly outnumbered by Corvettes at the Northampton Community College Show but a nice time was had by all. I went to the May Ford National at Carlisle and the following week went to the Wind Gap Show which I left early to get homemade ice cream at the Jacktown Show.

On the 8th of June, our club had a combined tour, picnic and real country hayride, and later that week my son Rob and I flew to Dearborn to Ford's 100th Anniversary. Washington, NJ had a parade on July 4th, Easton PA had its Heritage Festival the following week and then it was International Harvester's 100th bash at Bloomsburg Fairgrounds with 840 antique tractors. My old Farmall H included!

August brought the Warren County and Blue Valley Fairs and on September 6th it was Victorian Days at Belvidere and the very next day a private "by invitation only" show in Cresco. This was like it was in our club in the 1960's when members just brought a covered dish and the host family had its very own car show. The Washington Crossing, NJ show was held on the 19th through the 21st and was well attended.

Fall Carlisle started on October 3rd and Alpha, NJ had a nice little car show on October 5th and then Hershey was October 8th through 12th. On October 11th, I managed to get in the Crayola 100th Anniversary Parade since they needed an open vehicle to haul the inflatable green crayon man. My 1951 Chevy pickup just fit the bill. It was estimated that 10,000 people watched the parade, which was very well organized, but I saw only 4 porta potties. The next day there was a good car show at Northampton, PA and then I hurried back to Palmer Twp. Library for our October meeting.

I did miss our Region's Tour on October 26th but got to the last show of the year at Riegelsville. Arriving at 8:40 am, we were told that the 4-acre show ground was full and we had to park in the alley. There certainly are a lot of antique cars and a lot of car nuts in the area and we -- our Lehigh Valley AACA Region-- can't even get any new young members!

Another Flood

"You get in the boat first, I'll hand the baby to you and then I'll get in," Art said. His neighbor had rowed out in the swiftly-rising muddy water to rescue the family, just as in the Johnny Cash song "How high's the water Momma?" The family had discussed their options and eventually moved their belongings up the central stairway to the second floor as the water continued to come up higher. They really did not have too many possessions. They had been married only a year and a half when they had rented this farm along the river. The barn was up on the hill so the animals would be safe, but the house was in the bottomland.

Kneeling on the front porch roof and holding onto the bow of the rowboat with one hand, Art handed the kid to his wife and scrambled in. Art couldn't swim. Mr. Rapp rowed back to the nearest high ground, which was the Bel-Del Railroad right of way. Mrs. Rapp had graciously sent word that the family could stay with them until the water receded.

The next day – a complete mess! Plaster coming off of the laths, mud on every stair step, the cook stove dripping water, floorboards buckled, the rug a soggy mess. Outside the privy was upset, the hole a stinking danger. In fact, everything stunk. Logs and sawed lumber were everywhere. The saw mill was intact but the mill wheel and race were damaged. Art's corn crop was still underwater with pumpkins rotting everywhere. Somebody upstream must have planted a lot of pumpkins, which floated downstream and got caught in a backwater here.

Nobody could remember a flood like this. It all happened so suddenly. Of course it had been raining hard off and on for a week but no one expected a flood. And since the Delaware River was so high, the Pohatcong Creek backed up and created a backwater where the pumpkins lodged.

Renting this farm had seemed like such a good idea. The house was decent and the rent fair. The landlord was honest and it was a chance for the young couple to start out on their own. Art also could grind his cow feed when the waterpower was not needed to run the saw mill, which stood, next to the farmhouse. Mary Francis had enthusiastically papered the downstairs and fixed up a room for the baby upstairs. Now she had even lost her garden. A whole year's work for nothing and they had no money. Their savings had gone into field equipment and fixing up the house. They were penniless and distraught.

Since there was no other alternative, they moved all their belongings a mile and one half and moved in with Art's parents, Isaac and Charlotte. Two men on a farm is like two women in a kitchen and is not the best arrangement but they made the best of it and it worked for ten years until Art and Mary Francis could afford to build their own home; A brick two-story "American four square" on the farm. Actually, the family arrangement has worked for over one hundred years for six generations.

* The house that was flooded burned down about twenty years ago and the Rapp sawmill no longer stands just west of the iron railroad bridge on River Road, Pohatcong Township. My wife and I lived in that "American four square" today (up on a hill a mile from the Delaware) that my grandparents built and, oh yes, that infant rescued from the second story during the 1903 "pumpkin" flood was my father Harry H. Frey.

April Fool

Somebody built a new automobile museum in the Arbogast & Bastian Meat Packing Plant in Allentown.

I've visited quite a number of car museums over the years. Last winter Trudy and I visited one in Tupelo, Mississippi, Elvis Presley's birthplace. A collector who made his money in the broadcasting business set up a non-profit "Educational" Foundation to "shelter" his six-million-dollar collection in a 3-acre building. Among the 150 cars on display were an 1896 Benz, a purple 1939 Nash, a Tucker and lots of vehicles I had only read about. (Remember the Tallahatchie Bridge song? You cross en route to Tupelo).

Last fall, my wife and I took a "geezer" bus tour of the Pacific Northwest and got to visit a car museum in Idaho. There they also had one-hundred-fifty cars parked bumper to bumper, running board to running board, so close together that nobody ever even dusted them. This small museum had acquired many of those vehicles at a United States Government Internal Revenue Service Auction. It seems that the owner, a Mr. Tow, had forgotten to pay income tax on the profits from his Ford New Car Franchise because he was too busy collecting and restoring Antiques. There is a moral here and it has to do with April 15 every single year.

Hill Air Force Base

It seems hard to believe that cars manufactured in 1992 now qualify as antiques. Just a few years ago some purists looked down their noses at the muscle cars but now they are accepted, welcomed and covered in the AACA's new and improved bi-monthly glossy magazine.

Trying to define what an antique airplane is, is quite another story. There are lots and lots of planes over forty years old that are still flying. My neighbor (and fellow Lehigh Valley Region member) Frank Becker is a pilot and knows lots more about this than I do.

Trudy and I had an opportunity to visit the Hill Air Force Base in Utah this January where they restore military aircraft. One ten-acre hanger deals solely with rebuilding the landing gear assemblies. Each mechanism is dismantled, stripped of old paint, miked up, (micrometer) magnafluked and x-rayed to determine if it can be reused. The nation's largest x-ray machine is located here also. All this info goes into computer controlled lathes, grinders and milling machines that machine the parts as necessary so they can be re-bushed up to original specs. The components are reassembled, painted white, tested, crated up and shipped back to airbases world-wide.[1]

Another ten-acre building is a restoration shop par excellence. They strip down aging but still great F-16 fighter jets right down to the main frame. It is a frame off restoration if there ever was one. F-16's were designed before computers and were basically over designed. Bulkheads and panels are replaced as necessary and all wiring is replaced with 21st century technology. The cockpit is set up so there is a head's up digital display of the instrument panel on the pilot's face shield. New unit modules are plugged into the plane to accomplish the upgrades. All this is then done on a disassembly/reassembly line by Air Force Specialists and civilian employees in house although repro panels are farmed out to fabricators since Fairchild Company, which built F-16's no longer exists. After three months, the fighter jets come off the reassembly line far better than new.[2] For once, it seems that the government can do something right.

[1] The landing gear on a C-3 airplane is absolutely huge – as big as a Lincoln Navigator.

[2] The Air Force plans to continue using F-16 fighters to year 2025.

Food Glorious Food

There is a man named Dale,
Who is most hardy and hale
Living on truffles, key lime pie and cheese cake.
Lobster, turtle soup and flank steak
But refuses to eat any kale.

There is a man named Piccard
Whose doctor made it so hard
Living on veggies and greens
No sausage biscuits- just beans
And he absolutely hates rhubarb

Blue Heeler

There is a man here at Frey's
Whose blue Heeler dog will atomize
Dog food and cat poo she will vandalize,
And eat soggy crust from rhubarb pies,
But will not eat McDonald's French fries.

Cat

Cat is at the door
Wanting in, or
Wanting out some more,
Let her out, afore
Again she pukes on the floor.

Stuff

People collect stuff. It comes naturally going back to hunter-gatherers, and it is imprinted in the collective Broca brain of humanity. It is particularly strong in those of us who grew up in the Great Depression, when we coveted what little we had and probably still have.

Antique car nuts tend to collect big stuff like spare engines, but other kind of nuts collect cast iron manure spreader seats, milk bottles, paper weights, ash trays with tiny rubber tires, political buttons, (Hillary?), arrow heads, rocks, toys, coins, money, shot glasses, things with black and white Holstein spots, crucifixes, Mad Magazines, autographs, thimbles, baseball cards, mounted insects, stamps, ruby fishing lures, stuffed toy animals, (anybody remember Honey Kern?), AACA t-shirts and all kinds of knick-knacks.

Mrs. Huntington was a nice elderly lady who asked my wife and I how we met. She knew my wife was from Philly and I was from the Pohatcong Hills. So we told her. Then we asked her why she asked. Her reply was, "Some people collect salt and peppers shakers, ceramic figures, snow globes, etcetera; which just collect dust. I however collect information!"

* * * * * * *

Plastic

Baffles this hick
I can see what is inside,
But no matter how I tried,
I can't open it without a machete
Or a bayoneti.
Socks, magazines, food stuffs and tools
All shrink-wrapped for us fools
Baloney, concrete nails to dinner pails.
Toys, toilet paper made by Charmin
Repairs for stuff we broke while farmin'
Encapsulated, hermetically sealed
Until the plastic is totaled peeled
Like cosmetics by Mennen
Or the tomb of Vladimir Lenin

Tumble Turds

Oh Where, oh where have the dung beetles gone?
Oh Where, oh where can they be?
With backs so shiny and legs so tiny
That they all have gone missing disappeared into ignominy
How come? Were they dumb?
Like Neanderthals driven up walls by Homo sapiens
Who are always at fault (and drink too much malt)
But shite bugs had smarts by following carts,
Then pushing medicine balls up hills.
By being quite wise they got exercise and by eating got their tummies quite full.
The work they did love with push pull and shove
So just why is it they are on the endangered list
Sierra club's Jeff Tittle insists that they are so little
The post moderns blew them away
With voluminous tracts of alternative facts.
Elitists in their tedium forgot about Ford's vanadium.
Dung beetles disappeared when they heard
The rattles so near.
Their demise came to be
With the advent, you see,
Of Henry Ford's Model T.

Volvo-holics

Some guys bleed red for Case International and others bleed green for John Deere's. Likewise, there are avid Ford and Chevy truck fans and, of course, those black smoker Dodge enthusiasts who can't be ignored. Same is true with Sam who is a Volvo guy and has had several. In 1979, he bought a new left-over 1978 Volvo 780.[1] After the 1973 oil embargo. GM, in an effort to downsize their cars, put Cadillac trim on Chevettes and the Swedes tried to make the brick-shaped 240 into the luxury 780 Volvo. It didn't even have a V8 engine, just a small V6, but it had really fancy real walnut interior, an imitation-canvas hardtop and four heated, real leather seats.

Sam commuted to Trenton daily and put 280,000 miles on this car.[2] When he retired, the Volvo became the farm errand car and was parked outside. One night he noticed a faint glow outside. Next morning, he discovered the heated leather passenger seat had roasted itself and smoked up the entire interior. Sam had kept $100 deductible insurance on the car all these years.[3] The adjuster paid him $300 and told him to junk it. Sam advertised it on EBay and described his 780's condition fairly. To his surprise he got a call from a guy in Colorado who offered Sam $600 sight unseen and who had a friend in Pennsylvania with a trailer who would come pick it up and pay in cash.

Moral to the story... Don't throw anything away!

* * * * * * *

[1] Volvos were made and sold in Europe in the 1930's and by 1950 started to come to America to compete with the VW rear engine bug. They were expensive economy cars, with styling consistently ten years behind Detroit but were always ahead of the industry in safety features.

[2] There is a red Volvo P1800 coupe with over three million miles still in use.

[3] Volvo owners are considered a bit eccentric, and us Freys have owned five.

Little Brown Church

If you are going to the church by the cemetery
A Saturday-night bath is mandatory,
Then merrily go off to the stock car races
And you will come home late with dirty faces,
Covered with grease, clay and calcite,
You really should do what is right,
And take another bath tonight.
But just crawl between the sheets so clean
And wake up with dirty, greasy linen
So Sunday off to church you go,
And nobody will ever know.
Amen

A Poem

Some of the great things

That the fifties did bring

Were detergent oil

Styling by Harley Earl

The greatest name in power steering.

Charlie

Charlie was an air force mechanic during the Korean War, servicing the multiple magnetos on 27-cylinder air-cooled Pratt and Whitney aircraft engines. He was transferred to being a flight mechanic on a B-36. (1

On a flight to Europe, gauges indicated a problem in the right-side outside engine. The pilot ordered Charlie to crawl out through a tunnel that was in the wing itself and report back. The Pratt & Whitney engines needed supplemental cooling, and a bearing to the fan was red hot and about to catch fire. The pilot ordered everybody to bail out with the instructions to count to 10 before pulling the rip cord on the parachute (2)

Charlie had never jumped before, pulled the cord immediately, and survived. The others all drowned because the plane was so low at that point. Fortunately, it happened in the shipping lanes, and thirteen hours later he was picked up by a Russian freighter. They sent a guy down to tie a rope onto Charlie and hoisted him up. When they got on deck, the same guy was waiting, and to this day Charlie doesn't know how he got there.

This same guy wrapped him in a blanket and offered Charlie a drink to warm him up.

Charlie took one whiff and said, "No, thank you."

The Russian says, "Okay. I drink." And he threw it back like water.

* A special thank you to all the guys who risked their lives and lost their lives over the years.

(1) The B-36 had Pratt and Whitney engines on the back edge of the huge wings (pusher props).

(2) So the parachute wouldn't get entangled in the tail assembly.

URPS – 1, SAPS – 0

Cliff summed it up well when he spoke up at a Greenwich Township meeting: "If you people would go back to where you came from, we all would be better off." Some of the new Sophisticated Affluent People (SAPS) sometimes seem a bit of a pain to us Unsophisticated Rural Peasants (URPS).

Erv had a donkey, an old donkey he'd got when the kids were small. They had wanted a pony, but ponies can be really nasty, so he got a donkey and told the kids to imagine it had short ears. The kids grew up, and the donkey stayed. A family heirloom, a pasture mascot, it had plenty of H2O, hay, and grass to eat and spent its time under a shade tree along the county road.

One nice spring day, a well-dressed lady in a new BMW stopped by and told Erv that his donkey was being maltreated and neglected because its feet were bad, and she was going to call the SPCA. (1) Probably the woman had bad feet herself – maybe blisters, bunions, corns or hammer toes, and thus she felt sympathy for the poor old donkey.

After a few cuss words, Erv called a livestock dealer whom he knew well and ordered a gray donkey to be delivered before daybreak. He took the poor old lame one out behind the barn and shot it to put it out of its misery. Then he called Backhoe Joe to bury it back in the willows.

The next morning, two armed SPCA officers, the BMW lady, a couple of her do-gooder friends, and a New Jersey mass media reporter/photographer all arrived at Erv's farm and seemed a bit confused by what they found. You've seen one, you've seen them all. Happy Easter.

(1) In NJ, the SPCA is an agency to be feared: SPCA officers carry guns & have been known to seize pet rabbits without a warrant.

154

My Dogs

There is a book entitled *Why Dogs Chase Cars,* and basically it says it's because they lack trigger finger and opposable thumbs to tie hangman's nooses or to turn on gas jets. Personally, I think they do it just for the thrill of it.

When I was a kid my Grandpa Frey had a German shepherd that chased cars. He caught one once or at least he caught the tire. He bit through a bald 4.25 x 19 (We are again back to 19-inch wheels in 2008) and hung on. It flipped him over, and the car ran right over his nose. Everyone thought this was pretty funny, except for the motorist with a flat tire, Grandpa, and old "Shep" who gave up chasing cars then and there.

I've had quite a few good dogs in my lifetime. As a kid, it was "Chippy" who would tear the house apart if he heard a mouse. Later there was "Bozo" who loved to ride on the operator's platform of our 1938 John Deere. We had "Nemo" who chased Goodyear Blimps until they disappeared over the horizon.

At one time, we had "Betsy", a nice Brittany Spaniel who patiently waited for our kids' school bus, but whose septic ears stunk so badly we could hardly stand it. Then there was "Dingo" that spent a lot of time licking his butt on the yellow line in the middle of the county road. He ended up just like "Patches" who had a habit of crossing Interstate 78. "Red Dog" was a really nice pet who just loved to ride in my '49 Chevy truck. His only vice was to go to the town of Alpha to visit the lady dogs. Then I would drive through the back alleys calling his name and blowing the horn. He would appear and after a good scolding show a lot more contrition than Elliot Spitzer. We had "Burkey" who could spot a groundhog a half mile away. "Lucky", "Perky" and "Penny" came later.

Somewhere along the line, a retiring farmer gave me a Border Collie. "Laddy" was supposed to round up cows, but all he really liked to do was chase barn cats. He would not bother with rats, mice or groundhogs and when our cat population got down to four, I decided to tell the previous owner to come get "Laddy" before I had to shoot him. Don't tell the PETA people that this idea even crossed my mind or they may take me away to the funny farm.

About 15 years ago I decided I really needed a good cow dog and got "John" a registered Australian Red Heeler from a breeder*. Somebody in Australia got the bright Idea to breed the single-minded, but wimpy Border Collies to Dingos. These Australian wild dogs spend their time chasing kangaroos and avoid getting kicked in the head. The result was a red, medium-sized dog that bred true.

"John" had a great sense of humor, knew over 30 words, loved to ride on my all-terrain vehicle, catch Frisbees, work with cattle and keep me company. We buried "John" on Palm Sunday behind the barn in a bed of straw with his toys and a Frisbee. And, he never, ever, chased cars.

*Cy Harker from Sussex NJ was a breeder of Red Heelers and fine horses. He was best known for teaching Roy Rogers and Gene Autry how to do trick horseback riding. He rode horseback all the way from Hollywood to Sussex County, NJ. He was probably the last of the true cowboys. It was a pleasure to meet him.

Countdown 3...2...1....

BLASTOFF!!

My Mom

My mother, Marian Hance Frey, was born in 1903, married during the Great Depression, and had me in 1931.

She was a working mother if there ever was one, but she worked at home and on the farm: cooking, cleaning, washing (Maytag putt-putt-putt), ironing and canning produce from her garden. You haven't really eaten well unless you have tasted home canned pork chops - and pies made from canned elderberries. She also fed the calves, carried milk from barn to milk house and scrubbed up the milking machines daily for years.

Her pin money was the egg money. Every March she got two hundred baby chicks (by U.S. mail) and raised them on home grown grains that my father ground with his John Deere tractor and Letz feed mill. The roosters were eaten or sold as broilers, and the hens were kept for the eggs. These eggs mother gathered, candled, graded, sorted and then delivered to her customers in town every Friday.

Sometimes folks only needed (or could only afford) six eggs, but mother always sold all her eggs or she traded them for groceries at the A & P Store.

One warm spring day in 1941, she was coming down Stockton Street hill and forced to slam on the brakes to miss a kid on a bicycle and thus dumped three big (Longaberger style) egg baskets off the back seat and on the floor of the 1931 Chevrolet two-door.

Marian Frey & Son
(Note the bib overalls.)

My mother was a happy, bright and intuitive person but this really spoiled her day and week. She went home, called all of her egg customers on the phone and apologized for the inconvenience. She then got the water hose and started to flush the omelet out of the car. The resulting mess ran under the front seats and out on the running boards and stuck fast. She tried everything she could think of — Fels Naptha, Rinso, Oxydol and even Lysol. My father came in from the fields and, being the Christian gentleman he was, told her it was alright — she had not hit the bicyclist and just not to worry.

But it wasn't alright. As summer came on so did the flies. Maggots grew in the joints where the fenders joined the running boards. By the time the really hot days of August arrived, the car smelled like sulfur dioxide and flies crawled all over the garage like they did when mother cooked sauerkraut in the kitchen.

Clearly something had to be done, so my father bought an almost new 1941 two-tone green Chevrolet Special Deluxe Sedan from a young man who had enlisted in the Marines. World War II soon broke out, and the Frey family had a "new" car for five whole years. The 1931 Chevy was readily sold (smell and all) and was occasionally seen up until VJ Day in 1945. Oh yes, mother always carried her egg baskets in the trunk of the car henceforth.

Harry Frey hosing off the 1931 Chevrolet

My Dad

He was a good man. Far better than I, and I figured this out at an early age. He was religious and sang in the church choir for 70 years with a clear, strong baritone voice. He was a good mechanic, a patient man, and I never once heard him swear. He was a farmer and farmers have a lot to cuss about. But he never once did. He did mutter sometimes under his breath and with me around he had a reason to do so. He and I worked together almost daily for forty years (with and for each other). I miss him and his advice although at times I must admit I did not relish or welcome his advice. Looking back on it now, I guess he was usually right and I'd like to share this story about what and all right guy he was.

Harry...

Things were scarce on the home front during World War II. On the farm we had plenty of food and could get gasoline for the tractor, but my father never put a drop of it in the car. He had an 'A' ration stamp for the car and bought his allotment at the local gas station. About the only place we went was to Old Greenwich Church. The car tires were poor and he "made do" with second-hand recaps and blow-out patches.

The Lang and bolster broke on dad's hay wagon, so he went to the ration board and got approval to buy a whole new farm wagon running gear. He ordered it from the Sears & Roebuck catalog, and when it came by Railway Express it had four brand new B. F. Goodrich passenger car tires mounted on the wheels. Nobody had seen new car tires for over three years, but my father put them on his hay wagon and there they stayed.

Our neighbor Ken's 1937 Chevy needed tires also. When he heard about my father's wagon tires, he got ration board approval and immediately ordered a Sears wagon. But his came with ribbed 6.00 x 16 front tractor tires (see picture) which he promptly put on his car and went to Ocean City. My dad thought it was totally improper to do such a thing, and I thought my dad was kind of stupid to leave new tires on a hay wagon. But now I know my father was a man Diogenes was looking for and I'm proud to be his son. If your dad is still around be sure to give him a hug this Father's Day.

This is the tractor upon which my father taught me to drive. He said I could drive it myself when I could start it.

Poetry?!

Ate an oyster, milked a camel
Rode a horse
Made a meal of a mealy bug
Or a slug
Or ate kale without fail.
Wish I could shake his hand
Or give her a hug
They should get the Nobel Prize
But they are fossilized
To those apes, Donovian or Neanderthals
We are in debt
To you-alls.
* * *

If the wife is shopping bent,

And to her some money you lent,

Or your VISA she did confiscate,

What to do while you wait?

Watch the pretty girls and placate.

* * *

A citizen of the good old U S of A
Arises every single day
A-feared of the SPCA*, DEP, COPD, U2S, NRCS and NSA
Also, DMV, DAR, Kim Young Gun, NBA, USDA, OMG, FBI,
LGBT
And our very own CIA

*In New Jersey, SPCA officials carry revolvers.

Obits

Are read everyday
About the good folks who just passed away
Their ages, job, education (standard format).
About their spouses and pet cat.
Were they scolds or gentle folk,
Whose likker was just Coke?

Who could take a (politically incorrect) joke
Or were they unhappy all the time?
And never thought to make a rhyme,
Like Sondheim while in their prime?

The reader will never know in his quest
Because he himself will turn around twice
And will be forgotten with the rest.

Our pet Midget on her 20th birthday

A Maize

Rows long and short
Knee high,
Ready for lay by.

Back and forth
The cultivator goes,
While I try not to doze.

Thanks to big pharma for 2 4-D,
This Farma discovered girls
At twenty-three.

Huh?

There once was a really old lout
To whom we had to shout
Conversations no use
His only excuse
His wife wore his hearing out.

1932: the Crime of the Century

By Dr. Bob Briglia

Charles Lindbergh came to New Jersey in 1932 to reclaim his privacy after five years of living as the most famous, most photographed and most admired man on earth. But instead of finding peace at his newly built estate in Hopewell Township, the hero aviator lost his infant son to a kidnap-murder that was instantly billed the most infamous crime in U.S. history.

The Lindbergh case of 1932 remains endlessly fascinating. It offers the heartbreak of a baby's death, the detective drama that led to Bruno Hauptmann's arrest two years later—and the intriguing, if unproved, theory that the authorities may have executed the wrong man.

But before there was a Lindbergh case or a Lindbergh baby, becoming a public idol was the furthest thing from young Charles mind. He just wanted to land in one piece. On May 20, 1927, Lindbergh determined to fly the Atlantic, New York to Paris, in a stunt that wowed the public as a daring dash against all odds. He had no radio, no co-pilot and no precedents-for no one had ever attempted to cross an ocean alone. When he landed "the Spirit of St. Louis" at Paris' Le Bourget airfield, after 34 hours of nonstop flying from New York, he was an instant hero.

Lindbergh, a shy, unpretentious Minnesota boy was only 25 at the time of his record-breaking flight. He did not posture or publicize himself. But his very modesty only seemed to make him that much more of a hero.

On a goodwill flight to Mexico City soon afterward, he met his future wife, Anne Morrow, daughter of a prominent New Jerseyan who was ambassador to Mexico. In 1930, the newly-wed Lindbergh's had a baby, Charles Jr. His birth was front page news everywhere, but the family shunned all publicity and shielded themselves from prying eyes by retreating to a new home. They bought a 425-acre tract in the remote Sourland Mountains, 14 miles north of Trenton, at a site Lindbergh personally selected by flying overhead. Surrounded by thick woods and hills and accessible only by a twisting dirt road, they settled into their dream house where they could raise their toddler son in peace.

On the night of March 1, 1932, the 20-month-old baby was kidnapped-there were few clues- a crudely made ladder and a ransom note for $50,000. On May 12th, the baby's body was found in the woods just four miles from the Lindbergh home. It took two and one-half years for the police to catch a break in the vase and on September 19, 1934, Bruno Richard Hauptmann was arrested.

In January 1935, Hauptmann went on trial in Flemington, NJ (the venue was Hunterdon County, not Mercer County, because a check of deed maps proved that while the front door of the Lindbergh property was in Mercer County, the nursery itself where the crime occurred was over the county line in East Amwell). More than 10,000 people surrounded the Main Street courthouse on days of especially dramatic testimony. Walter Winchell, Damon Runyon, Edna Ferber and Dorothy Kilgallen were among the celebrities covering the event for the New York papers. The trial had a hero and a villain. The hero was Lindbergh, who came to the trial every day. The villain was the foreigner Hauptmann.

Hauptmann was found guilty of murder on February 13, 1935m and sentenced to die in the electric chair. Following the trial, Charles Lindbergh, feeling embittered and hounded, deserted his Hopewell estate with his family for a new home in England- seeking not simply privacy, but isolation.

* * * * * *

A couple of months ago, I noticed an article in the Hunterdon Democrat Newspaper, that they were planning the re-enactment of the Lindbergh Child murder trial for October 10,2010. For years I have seen ads each year when they were going to do the same at the original courthouse in Flemington, NJ and I just did not follow up on it. This year, for some reason, I decided to go to Flemington to talk to Curtis Leeds, the editor of the Hunterdon County Democrat and the Warren Reporter, as my Packard belonged to Dwight Morrow, who was Anne Morrow Lindbergh's father. Mr. Leeds told me that this was the 20th year of re-enacting the trial and was going to be the last one. The Lindbergh's were transported to the trial in the Packard.

It was a great experience, one of the best in the 37 years I have been showing the car. The play was superb, the actors riveting, and the car drew a great deal of attention, because it was a direct connection to the original trial- it was there.

-     Dr. Bob Briglia

Old Cider Mill along Pohatcong Creek. Painting by Sandy Hager

1933 Packard V-12 Cabriolet DeVille-

The Most Elegant Packard designed by Fernandez-Darrin, Paris

by Robert D. Briglia

It was my good fortune to know Mr. Russell Lewis, one of the founders and first Vice-President of the Classic Car Club of America. Russ Lewis was the first "Master of the Grand Classic" held at Washington's Crossing, NJ on July 12, 1953. At the time Russ was an Armour Meat Company salesman in the northwest NJ area. Russ worked weekends in a small supermarket in my hometown of Alpha, NJ. Stating in 1948, as a teenager I worked in that supermarket as a stock boy and bagger. I had come to love old cars as there were many around during WWII and everyone worked to keep them running, as new automobiles were not available due to the war effort. Many of the Classics and antique autos were lost to the need for metal.

Russ would frequently bring one of his cars to work during the warm weather months. His cars included: 1933 Packard 12 (1006) Cabriolet DeVille by Fernandez-Darrin; 1932 Packard 12 convertible Victoria by Dietrich; 1931 Pierce-Arrow Silver Arrow convertible by LeBaron; 1934 Packard Standard 8, 4-door convertible and 1936 Ford 4-door convertible Roadster (nc).

At every possible opportunity, I would remind Russ that I wanted to have the Dietrich Convertible Victoria. It was a stunning car, with a hood that went on forever. He always advised me that he wanted his son, Lowell, to have them. After high school, I went on to Temple University School of Pharmacy, but continued to work part-time in the market, and of course kept in contact with Russ Lewis. Soon, my career as a Pharmacist began and I did not see Russ for a few years. In 1965, I opened a second pharmacy in Alpha, NJ.

One day in 1965, to my surprise, Russ stopped at the Alpha Pharmacy, and asked if I was still interested in the Packard. Of course, I said yes. He advised me to meet him at Earle Eckel's (of Stanley Steamer fame and one of the founders of the Antique Automobile Club of America) Autogiro hanger in Washington, NJ. Earle Eckel was also one of the first Air Mail pilots. I was there early. When he opened the hanger door (really a large old barn), I walked over to the Dietrich Victoria Convertible, and he promptly advised me. "That's not the one, you'll take the Fernandez-Darrin; that's the best Packard ever built, but you have to promise me, that you will restore it right." Russ was a pretty stubborn guy, and I protested mildly that I loved the Dietrich, but I knew it was "take it or leave it." He continued to wish his son would be interested in the others, but told me his son was interested in Pontiac GTO's, and he just could not understand it. It was clear he was only offering me the Fernandez-Darrin, and I am eternally grateful. I did tell him I was interested in purchasing all the others, if he changed his mind, but later he sold them to a dealer on the spur of the moment, and never called me. When I asked about it later, he said, "You have the best Packard ever built and you will need money to restore it right."

I was surprised by Russ' demand of me, to promise to restore the car, as Russ always believed the cars should remain in their original condition. However, after years of being involved in Grand Classics, Russ mellowed on the subject. Russell was the organizer of the first Caravan to Detroit in 1953. Lowell Lewis, then a 17-year-old, told me recently, he drove the car in shifts with his mother and father, and they experienced absolutely no problem on the trip.

Russell Lewis had acquired the Packard in 1951 from Coughlin Funeral Home in Califon, NJ (Hunterdon County). In 1974, after the restoration had been completed, I drove the car to Califon so that Mr. Coughlin could see it. I was also interested in the passenger compartment, or any information on the trunk, which I had not restored as yet. He loved seeing the car again and told me the story of how he acquired it.

Mr. Coughlin said the original owner was Senator Dwight Morrow, a New York Corporate Attorney, with a distinguished career. His firm represented several large corporations including Standard Oil of New York (ESSO), Packard New York and Union Valve (a company that belonged to Howard (Dutch) Darrin's family). Dwight Morrow was also a U.S. Senator from New Jersey and an Ambassador. Mr. Coughlin advised me, Senator Morrow's daughter, Anne was married to Charles Lindbergh. Dwight Morrow's wife was from a prominent family in New York (he mentioned the Tammanys). I have found most of this information to be true. Mr. Coughlin was getting up in years. I did not know how accurate the information would be.

Evidently, Senator Morrow wanted a new Packard 12, for his personal use, and wanted a body designed by Howard (Dutch) Darrin, who had relocated to Paris, France, due to the lack of demand for special bodied cars in the U.S.A. due to the depression. Initially, Dutch Darrin and Tom Hibbard worked for the New York firm of LeBaron. Hibbard was one of the partners, and Darrin was their representative in Paris. In the latter part of the 1922, they left LeBaron and formed Hibbard and Darrin of Paris and successfully designed bodies for General Motors, Rolls-Royce and others. In 1928, Hibbard and Darrin parted. Darrin decided to stay in Paris and formed a partnership with a French banker named Fernandez, and the Fernandez-Darrin Company was formed. As quoted from Robert Turnquist's definitive book, *The Packard Story,* "the partnership was responsible for some of the most eloquent body styles to ever grace a luxury chassis" and "the most elegant Packard designed by Fernandez-Darrin was a Tenth Series Twelve Convertible Sedan. It was long and low with a three-position top," which was "decaying in a damp garage and is unavailable to the real enthusiast." Russ Lewis and Bob Turnquist had a disagreement when they served together on the original Board of the Classic Car Club of America. As Russ told the story, he was in line to become the President of the club, but because Bob Turnquist had signed up more new members, the Board elected him President over Russ. As a result, Russ resigned from the Board. Later, I had an opportunity to discuss this with Bob Turnquist, but he denied the story.

The Morrows had a summer home in Oldwick, NJ. When a German U-Boat fired on the eastern coast, Mr. Morrow became concerned they would attack New York and moved to Oldwick for the duration of WWII.

166

The Morrows and their house-staff and chauffeur moved to Oldwick. Mrs. Morrow also had her own Packard, but Mr. Coughlin could not remember the model.

The cars were always chauffeur driven and maintained and garaged. Mr. Morrow would be driven into New York three or four times a week to conduct business, always returning to Oldwick.

Unfortunately, Mr. Morrow became ill and died before WWII ended. Mrs. Morrow refused to use "his car". At the time Mr. Coughlin was in dire need of a vehicle for his mortuary business. New vehicles were not available. He begged Mrs. Morrow to sell the Fernandez-Darrin to him and after some time she relented.

He promptly had the vehicle repainted with several coats of black lacquer. The trunk was recovered in black oilcloth. However, prior to repainting, he had a hole cut into the back of the car and the trunk. By pushing the trunk forward against the body with a sealing gasket, and removing the back seat, he was able to use the vehicle to transport bodies; a bit morbid but extremely interesting history. He also had a canvas cover made that stretched over the passenger compartment, allowing it to be used as a flower car. On weekends, he would pop the back seat into the car and head to the shore with his family. He recalled his daughter as a 4- or 5-year-old riding in the back seat, calling out to him as they were rounding the corner, "Daddy wait for me." I can imagine to a small child it was a long way back in that rear seat.

Of course, I was interested in information about the clock and the trunk. Mr. Coughlin advised me the trunk was filled with Louis Vuitton luggage and that it had a beautiful gold filigreed clock in the dash on the passenger compartment. My hopes soared when he told me he thought they still had the luggage and clock in the attic. He promised to ask his wide. He called me a few weeks later and said they were, unfortunately, gone. His wife had reminded him that he had given the luggage to his young daughter to plat with and store her dolls; and the clock was given to his son, and they were gone. It is interesting, however, that he help the original piece of metal that was cut out of the back of the car, and Russell Lewis kept it, and gave it to me when I purchased the car. That piece of metal was welded back into it original position. We only had to replace two wood supports, and repair the back of the trunk with new wood. Mr. Coughlin told me he had sold the car to Russell Lewis for $50.00.

In late 1969 or early 1970, Paul Marut, of Parkside Motors, Phillipsburg, NJ began restoring the Packard, which he completed in late summer of 1973. Paul was a well-known Cadillac restorer and information resource. His knowledge of all old cars was excellent, but he relied on others, such as Bob Turnquist and Jim Tuschinsky for information and parts. The engine was restored by Rollin Peters of Bethlehem, PA (who was a specialist in Lycoming engines used in Duesenbergs). Rollin was in his mid to late 80's when he restored the engine. It was beautiful, to see the engine stat immediately on the first try. Rollin died a few months short of his 100th birthday. His machine shop was a marvel and he was a gem.

The Packard was first shown in Hershey in 1973, where it won a first prize. At the Grand Classic in Cherry Hill in 1974, it won first prize and best of show. Over the years, it has won many first prizes, and is a senior. In 1978 the Packard Fernandez-Darrin was invited to the Concours d'Elegance at the New York Coliseum where it was selected as "Best Classic Car." For many years my career as a physician (I had left pharmacy in 1972 to return to medical school) did not allow me enough time to prepare the car for shows, so I limited myself to local shows.

The Packard Centennial and the Opus Magnum encouraged me to contact Jim Tuschinsky to go over the engine. Unfortunately, Jim died suddenly before he could complete the task. Fortunately, Rich Fass of Stone Barn Restorations in Vienna, reassembled the engine and completed a few cosmetic repairs. The car was late invited to Pebble Beach Concours, where it won third prize, approximately 27 years after restoration.

Bob Turnquist refers to his automobile in his excellent book, *The Packard Story* as "the most elegant Packard designed by Fernandez-Darrin." It has been a joy to show the car over many years and enjoying the pleasure it gives so many interesting people who come to shows.

Behind Our Outhouse

It was late in the afternoon of New Year's Eve when Furman hunted me up. He and Louise were the tenants in the old farm house and were expecting company for a big New Year's Eve party AND the toilet was plugged up. Not only that but 'stuff' was backed up in the bath tub.

Now it should be pointed out that rural areas usually do not have sewers and rely on cesspools and/or septic tanks which have to be pumped out every couple of years. The solids are supposed to digest themselves and the fluids flow into a gravel bed* covered with topsoil where they are supposed to percolate into the soil or evaporate. Also, it is supposed to help the digestive system of the septic tank if you throw a dead rat or groundhog into the tank once in a while. I jumped into my pickup and got to the local rental agency just as the proprietor was closing. I rented a mud pump** and hurried back to the farm. We quickly unloaded the pump and were ready to pump out the septic tank.

But where to pump it to? Can't put it in the ditch along the county road and pumping it into the cow lot did not seem like a good idea. Then the light bulb flashed: pump it into the unused outhouse pit. A couple of buckets of water was not sufficient, so a water hose was used to prime the device. The intake hose went into underground tank, other hose down through the toilet seat. I asked Furman to hold the exhaust hose so it would not jump out and it worked, "Glug, glug, glug" just as it was supposed to do with mud. I was feeling pretty proud of myself when Furman yelled "Shut it off!" As it turned out, he got tired of leaning over the black abyss and peering in through the toilet seat; so he sat down on the other privy seat (a two-holer - His and Her's) and was almost asleep when he realized the stuff was coming up through the floorboards.

They had a lot to talk about at the New Year's Eve party.

* * * * *

* The gravel beds capacity was enlarged whenever we happened to have a dead cow: we would get "Backhoe Joe" to dig a hole at the end of the septic field, push the carcass in, dump in 10 tons of ¾ inch gravel and whoopee - two birds killed with one stone.

** Mud pumps are used to pump mud (obviously) out of foundations and construction sites, and I figured it would pump out semi-solids efficiently. Mud pumps come with a couple of fire hoses.

BANKING ON IT

First it was Bloomsbury Bank.
Then it was Citizens Bank.
Then it was Citizens National Bank.
Then it was Fleet Bank
Then it was Somerset Bank.
Then it was Summit Bank.
Then it was PNB.
Now it's PNC.
It's no longer a private bank.
It was once a family-owned bank
Established in the 1800's
When it was decided they needed a bank.
It eventually got to be a big, big bank,
Too big to fail.

LEXICOGRAPHY

A collection of obsolete and obsolescent words and expressions amassed by the late Norbert E. McGuire
Born: 11/4/31 - Died: 7/6/17

Norbert E. McGuire was responsible for this list of obsolete words which he complied in his last three months. We had become friends in grade school, kept in contact for 70 years, and shared many common interests including a love for words. He passed away July 6, 2017.

* * * * *

WIDESPREAD SAYINGS:

He looks be-shit – *one who walks stiff-legged and bent over, and looks as if he'd messed his pants*

Lock, stock and barrel – *the whole thing (ref. a rifle)*

The whole nine yards – *the whole thing (ref. a load of dirt)*

Cool – *approval or admiration; noun or adjective; now (21st Century) may be replaced by "hottie" for an attractive person*

Oh, my! Wow, Doozy, Super-dooper, Hotdog, Zoowy! – *expressions of amazement, approval*

Oh, Pshaw, Piffle, Fiddlesticks, Oh my goodness, What in tarnation, Confound it! Goodness sakes – *expressions of disappointment, disbelief, or belittlement*

Dad gum, Dadgummit, Dad blamed, Consarned – *polite cuss words*

Snooty – *stuck-up or conceited*

Snotty – *runny nose*

Drop-dead gorgeous, Eye-catcher, Sweetie Pie, Sweet britches – *attractive woman, number 10*

Fix'n, aim to do... - *getting ready to do something*

Run off – *escaped or chased away*

Rar'n to go – *anxious to start*

Get gone, Hit the road, Get outta here. – *going somewhere*

A bridge too far – *gone beyond reasonable expectations*

Run hard and put away wet – *from horse and buggy days, failure to take proper care of your horse; now, failing to take care of your tools or equipment.*

Well, dog mah cats, if'n it hain't – *recognition of a surprise visitor, as in: "Well dog mah cats if'n it hain't Bob Frey a-comin' up th' lane."*

You guys, them guys, youse guys – *slang pronouns*

Rank & Faiole – *military formation, also a group*

Hear tell, heerd – *past tense of hear*

Seed – *past tense of see*

Your'n, his'n, her'n, my'n – *possessive pronouns*

Deviltry – *politically incorrect teasing*

Tormenting – "

Practical jokes – "

Stunts – "

Not no more – *never again*

It don't make no never mind. – *It doesn't matter.*

That's a no-no. – *forbidden*

Cuts no ice, If you say so… - *doubtful*

Butt in – *unwelcome*

Cuts the mustard – *satisfies*

Bite the dust, Deader'n a doornail, Deader'n hammer, He jus' up'n died, Graveyard dead – *deceased*

Night owl – *one who stays up late at night*

Locked and loaded – *prepared to open fire*

Joint – *a bar or restaurant of low esteem*

Out – *as in 'It's raining out, sunny out, cold out, I'm going out, the fire went out, out of gas*

Kilroy was here – *graffiti from WWII*

Run around like a chicken with its head cut off. – *bizarre behavior*

Outlandish – "

Gone 'round the bend – *crazy*

Teched in th' hed (haid) – "

Off his rocker – "

Nut case, wacko – "

One quarter-bubble off – "

Not all his marbles – "

Bats in his belfry – "

Goofy – "

Pig on ice – *clumsy*

Chip on shoulder – *anxious to fight*

Booby hatch – *asylum for the deranged*

Woozy – *dizzy, dazed*

Beast or critter – *a cow or other animal*

Varmint – *a pest or small animal such as rats and mice*

Jined – *joined, jointed*

Coonass – *a cracker/redneck*

A coon's age – *a long time*

Fambly, Fably, Kith and Kin, Kissin' Cousins, kinfolks – *family*

Ticked off – *annoyed*

Tellwiddott,The Hell with it – "

Rubbed the wrong way – "

Dear – *high-priced*

Gumption – *initiative*

Shiftless – *lazy, inefficient*

Lazy bones – *lazy*

Chew the fat – *idle talk*

Hogwash – "

Stood around and groused about it – "

Tongue-lashing – *scold*

Hue and Cry, Barking the loudest – *yell and holler*

Hem and haw – *indecisive talk*

Blow hard – *talks too much*

Wind bag - *talks too much*

Kibosh – *to put an end to*

Galoshes – *rubber overshoes*

Galluses, Braces – *suspenders*

MacIntosh – *heavy plaid jacket*

Tart – *unpleasant woman*

Women's work – *chores commonly performed by women*

Smartass – *wise guy*

Snotty – *a nasty wise person*

Stingy – *tight-fisted, thrifty*

Spilt, spilled – *as in 'No use in crying over spilt milk."*

A-feared – *afraid*

Willies – *nervous, scared*

Short end of the stick – *loser*

Shitty end of the stick – "

Hind tit – "

Sore loser – "

Cranky pants – *whiny loser*

Sore-ass – "

Spats – *linen to cover shoes, also family fights*

Bilious – *sick from excess bile, greenish-yellow skin*

Front room, parlor – *living room*

Davenport - *sofa*

Glider – *swing*

In a pig's eye – *unlikely*

Bare as a bear's behind, bare-assed naked – *naked*

They're an item – *couple*

Hitched – *married*

Fart in a mitten – *run around aimlessly*

Fart in a bottle – "

Fart high in a windstorm – "

Fart in a hurricane – "

Mosey along – *walk leisurely, saunter*

Chuck-a-block – *full*

Ain't so hungry as I was before I et – *full*

Contrary – *in opposition or denial, willful*

Ham-handed – *clumsy*

Upside of the head with a 2x4 – *to strike a hard blow*

Warts and all – *to accept, even with imperfections*

Spavin-legged – *a lame horse or person*

Yuge – *misspelling of Huge commonly on the internet today*

Lipstick on a pig – *futile attempt to beautify*

Bamboozle – *to trick*

Fickle – *often changing, disloyal*

Snit – *agitated state*

All beside myself – *flustered*

Tizzy – "

Tougher than a pig's snout – *very tough*

Tougher than a boiled owl – "

Rough as a cob – "

Opine – *express an opinion*

Wheels are turning – *hard thinking underway, things are happening*

Slick, slick as a whistle – *smooth*

Pussy-footed – *sneaky like a cat*

Gravy train – *free stuff*

Head cahots, head honcho – *in charge, most important*

King pin – "

Grand Poohbah – "

In cahoots – *in collaboration with*

Hot head – *one easily offended*

Finagle – *to behave or obtain dishonestly*

Boondoggle – *trivial, unnecessary work*

Pencil pusher, paper pusher – "

The door yard – *back yard*

Winders – *windows*

Fair to middlin' – *a reply to greeting, "How are you?"*

Toler'ble – "

Clinker – *a fused cylinder, a bad mistake*

Chitlins – *remainder after rendering lard*

Chimbley – *chimney*

Ak-a-me – *ACME grocery store*

Pissin' in the wind – *wrong way*

Bass Ackward – *wrong way, useless*

The hurrier I go, the behinder I get – *haste makes waste*

Rug rats – *little kids playing on the floor*

Six to one, half-dozen to the other – *a dilemma, undecided*

Dancing around the subject – *beating around the bush*

Eight ways to Sunday – *every which way*

Let bygones be bygones – *Don't hold a grudge.*

Elevator don't go to the top – *odd*

Hill of beans – *small amount*

Pinch of shit – "

Smithereens – "

Brought down the house – *statement brought applause*

Wait up – *Wait for me, stay up 'til I get there.*

Stay put – *Don't move, don't leave.*

Whatchamacallit – *I can't think of the right word.*

A mark – *a sucker*

All hell broke loose – *a disaster occurred*

Out of kilter – *not properly adjusted*

Odd – *strange*

Neck of the woods – *parcel of land*

Spic and span – *clean*

To and fro – *back and forth*

Peepers – *Slang for eyes, frogs, frogs' mating calls*

Roundabout – *traffic circle*

Bother stone – *a rounded stone found in or near rivers*

Up the river – *in prison*

Up the crick without a paddle – *out of luck*

Up shit crick – "

Beeline – *straight or rapidly forward*

Hold down – *to keep*

Hold up – *to rob*

Stung – *cheated*

Fall – *Autumn*

Grapevine – *informal communications*

Pig in a poke – *unknown, to buy something without knowing what it is*

Slept like a log – *slept soundly*

Well, it's about time. – *finally receiving attention*

Short shrift – *receiving little attention*

Cord string – *lightweight string to fasten things*

Look it up – *research*

Roots around – *looking for something*

Mesmerized – *to enthrall, spellbound*

Like two piss-holes in a snowbank – *derogatory comparison of someone's eyes*

The Heartland – *States in the middle of USA*

How come...? – *Why*

Suck it up, buttercup. – *Take your lumps, and stop complaining*

It's clobberin' up fer rain. – *It's going to rain*

Raining pitchforks and hammer handles – *hard rain*

Raining cats and dogs – *hard rain*

Racist – *derogatory political term for your opponent*

Bronical tubes – *bronchial, branches of windpipe to lungs*

Hey, it could happen to anyone. – *plea of innocence*

What's going on out there? – *inquiry of some disturbance*

Cook stove – *coal or wood-fired stove in the kitchen*

Sick-a-bed on two chairs – *When any of my great-grandmother's nine kids got sick, she'd make a bed of two chairs a-front the cook stove to keep them warm. She made cough syrup from butter and brown sugar, simmered in vinegar on the cook stove. It worked good for the croup.**

The rich get richer and the poor have kids – *My great-grandparents raised nine kids with no running water, electricity or refrigeration. No social services, welfare, food stamps, Medicare or Medicaid. No Amend XVI to fleece the rest to pay for it. The old man always worked and the old lady took care of the kids. They went to church. They stayed married until they died in their late eighties. In their later years, the kids took care of them.**

[* Those two above refer to the Maguire family.]

Hung out to dry – *taking the blame*

The goat – *one who took the blame*

Tarred with the same brush – *guilty by association*

Get on the stick – *get going, take action*

Treading water – *barely keeping up*

Can't see the forest for the trees – *so concerned with details, you can't see the big picture*

That dog won't hunt – *the idea doesn't work*

Don't have a dog in the fight – *not interested in what's going on*

Laundry list – *a list of many concerns*

Many ways to skin a cat – *There are different ways to accomplish something*

To the nth degree – *carrying things to a fine point*

Hedging our bets – *taking precautions, buying insurance*

Jim Dandy, Jack Dandy, Jack Daniels – *just great*

Water it down, watered stock – *diluted, usually to create a false impression*

Now and then – *occasionally*

Took a shine to – *fond, like it, appreciate*

Sleepy head – *hard to wake up*

Lazy man's load – *trying to carry too much to avoid a second trip*

What's not in your head is in your heels – *You'll have to go back to get it*

You'd lose your head if it wasn't fast – *forgetful*

Raggle-tailed, raggle-ass, rag-tag – *looking poorly*

A ring-tailed snorter – *ferocious*

Liar, liar, pants on fire – *mocking someone caught in a lie*

Don't give a rat's ass – *unconcerned*

Keep your powder dry – *be prudent*

"Old Timey" – *nostalgic*

Dragging their heels – *reluctance*

Besotted, sozzled, drunk as a skunk – *drunk*

All shit-faced, pissy-ass, fallin'down drunk – *drunk*

Keen – *excellent, sharp, attracted to, sharp edge, intense*

Mind your manners – *be polite*

Mind your own self – *"*

Cuts the mustard – *That'll do it*

Too old to cut mustard anymore – *Can't do it*

Thicker'n molasses in January – *very slow moving*

Hotter than a Blue Bitch – *pretty hot*

Rats ran through your attic – *genealogy under suspect*

Looky here – *take a look*

Over Easton – *going to town (when there was something there)*

Tan my hide – *punishment*

Well, tan my hide! – *expression of surprise*

Skating on thin ice – *dangerous to proceed*

Sicker'n a dog – *very sick*

Giddy – *frivolous, flighty, spinning around*

Giddy Yup – *get going, horse*

Whoa – *stop horse*

Gee and Haugh – *fly by wire for horses*

Sunday-go-to-meeting – *dressed in our best clothes*

Autta – *should*

Penny wise and dollar foolish – *save and spend on the wrong things*

Poor as a church mouse – *very poor*

Get it thru your head – *Listen to what I'm telling you*

Blowing smoke – *fast talk to confuse the listener*

Stir up a hornet's nest – *cause trouble*

A-feast – *afraid to eat something (moldy, contaminated)*

Build a fire under it – *trying to get a mule going, or Fordson tractor moving (has actually been tried)*

AUTOMOTIVE:

Stove bolt – *hotrodder's term for Chevrolet or Chevy*

Pony-ack – *Pontiac*

An 88 – *a powerful Oldsmobile or Olds on Chevy chassis*

Big-ass Bur-ick – *a Buick according to some Black soldiers I knew*

Caddy – *Cadillac*

MOPAR – *acronym for Chrysler Corp.*

Plimit Baccarooda – *Plymouth Barracuda*

FoMoCo – *Acronym for Ford Motor Co.*

Sunday Ford – *Mercury*

Garage Man's Companion – *GMC, General Motors Corp.*

Jimmy – *a Chevy sold by Pontiac or Buick dealers*

Steady Breaker – *Studebaker*

NAPA – *acronym for No Auto Parts Available*

Jeep Station Wagon – *first of its kind – circa 1946, now called an SUV or crossover*

American Motors – *disaster following merger of Hudson and Nash*

Ford – *Found On Road Dead*

Purrs like a kitten – *motor runs smooth and quiet*

New Fangled – *new models, as in Edsel*

Clunker – a 'lemon' – *a car that always has something wrong*

DUTCHIFIED EXPRESSIONS:

It's all. – *all gone*

Oma or Opa – *Grandmother or Grandfather*

Ache! Spect nich so Dum! – *Don't talk so dumb.*

Grund Sau – *groundhog or woodchuck*

Aut – *out*

It wonders me. – *I wonder why, what, how…?*

Say not? – *Don't you agree? Right?*

Outen the light. – *Turn off the light.*

Juss fer nice. – *ornamental*

Et – *at*

Alles Kaput. – *done for*

Aye, aye, aye. – *astonishment*

The machine – *automobile*

All buggered up. – *bent, scratched, busted*

Leery – *suspicious*

NATIONALITIES:

Kraut – *German*

Yid – *Jew or Hebrew*

Bohunk – *from former Austro-Hungarian Empire*

Mick, Pady, Harp – *Irish*

Honky – *White person who honks his horn.*

Red Neck – *White Southern farmer*

Uker-ranian – *Ukrainian*

Polock – *Polish*

SAYINGS OF NORBERT'S NEIGHBOR, HARVEY

Burshel - *bushel*

Speed Thermometer - *His Studebaker had one*

Don't know nothin' 'toll about it, but a feller tol' me... - *opening statement before telling everything*

He'll never make a farmer 'long's he's got a hole in his ass...! – *estimate of his son's ability*

The Woman – *his wife*

Oh! Howard! – *(Annie) Will you shut up!*

Colder'n a witch's tit – *very cold*

Happy as a pig in shit (or a puddle) – *very happy*

S.O.S. – *shit on a shingle (creamed beef on toast)*

Fly door – *screen door to keep bugs out; often made of fancy wood moldings; held shut by a hook-eye*

Cut it half in two – *way to share the last piece of cake or pie*

Dumber'n the little red dog – *not too bright*

Dumber'n a box of hammer handles - "

Dumber'n dirt or a rock – "

Don't know his ass from a hole in the ground – "

Out to lunch – "

Bloomin' idiot – "

Meat head, Air head – "

Didn't have a clue – "

Idjet, Dunderhead – *not too bright; stupid*

Shiit poke – *street cleaner in horse and buggy days; a beetle; a derogatory expression for one who is useless [See page 147]*

THE IMPETUOUS FAMILY

Roy was a big strong farmer like in a Hastings piston ring ad. Back in the 1950's when we could still overhaul our own car engines over a weekend with some borrowed tools, Hastings ads featured tough but oh-so-gentle scenes with a big guy putting a little Tweetie bird back in its nest.

Roy's family had a pet turkey. It followed his wife around like a dog, picked the bugs out of the garden, and took the grain out of the cow manure. He and his wife had a bunch of kids - two girls and two boys – and the turkey would only take off after daughter Mel and bite her in the rear and swat her with its open wings. Roy's wife Maureen – they called her "Moo" like a cow - said, "Roy, you gotta be doing something about that. We can't have that turkey chasing us. You gotta do something about that." (1) One Sunday morning, Mel was all dressed up and in a hurry to teach Sunday-school when the turkey attacked her once too often. She went back in the house and got the shotgun, went back outside and splattered the turkey all over the sheets hanging on the line, returned the gun, and went off to teach her Sunday-school class. Later, her father said, "We think it's time you got your own place. (She was 20 years old and still living at home at the time).

Anyhow, with three men in the household, Roy's wife was saying, "You guys make an awful mess in this toilet. If you can aim a gun while hunting, you ought to be able to do a better job in the bathroom. You think that you can shoot, but you make a mess in the bathroom. And you're always leaving the lid and the seat up. You gotta do something about that. We can't have that." So, he got the saran wrap, and he very carefully wrapped the porcelain toilet bowl after which he put the seat down and the lid down.

He had rented another farm and convinced his wife that he needed a new tractor. He got a new John Deere 4020. Soon after that, he went to a farm sale where one identical to his new one was sold for half the price of what he had paid, so on the spur of the moment he bought that one too. Of course, his wife wasn't too happy about that, either.

Every day he drove his cows across the road to a pasture which had shade so they could drink out of the Musconetcong Crick (2) Now one morning a commuter pushed his way through the herd of cows and bumped a couple of them. Roy instantly took his cow stick (3) and beat on the hood of the commuter's car. Somebody called the state police. It just so happened that the trooper was a friend of Roy's (4) and he gave the commuter a ticket for hitting Roy's cows.

* * * * *

(1) *Frequently-heard wifely expression.*
(2) *This was before the NJ Department of Environmental Protection decided that cows shouldn't wade or soak their feet in the crick.*
(3) *A sawed-off broom handle.*
(4) *Loved to shoot groundhogs at Roy's.*

More Lost Arts

Of wearing galluses
Of wearing galoshes
Of mending socks
Of making a proper cup of tea
Of whittling
Of making souse
Of chivalry
Of harnessing a team
Of contrition
Of gigging for eels
Of eating chitlins
Of investigative reporting
Of callithumping[1]
Of practical jokes
Of caponizing cockerels
Of credibility
Of greasing one's own car
Of political incorrectness
Of making change
Of saying grace

1. A noisy serenade (made by banging on pans and
    kettles) to a newly married couple.
    (See page 7)

* * * * * * *

MISSY

Forty years ago, Missy's grandparents had a farm and she spent every summer there. She just loved the life, and she wanted to marry a farmer.

After high school and college, she got a job as a milk tester. New Jersey Dairy Herd Improvement Association had a tester who went 30 different farms a month and sampled milk from every single cow and weighed it, and tested it for butter fat so they could know which were good cows and which were poor cows and how to figure out the rest.

Anyway, she worked in Warren County and didn't find any farmers that were satisfactory. She left and went to New Zealand where there were a lot of farms. She milked cows for somebody there for two years and then came back to the states as she couldn't find any farmer in New Zealand who was satisfactory.

Her married friends convinced her that she was going to be an old maid and that she had to do something. She was pushing 30, an attractive redhead, a little on the chunky side, rather buxom, and had a great sense of humor. Her friends convinced her to put an ad in Hoards Dairyman Magazine. It's a bi-weekly newspaper for farmers and serves the dairy community across United States. She placed an ad that said: "Tall, fun-loving redhead wishes to meet dairy farmer." She got a couple calls, and she went to meet them, and they weren't satisfactory - not that she was being terribly fussy, but they just weren't satisfactory.

Then she got a call from a guy whose buddies convinced him to answer the ad. They were picking on him, kidding him about it, telling him that he was going to end up an eccentric bachelor farmer like Garrison Keillor's bachelor farmers...he was going to end up like that and live on potato soup and canned peaches.

So he called her, and they met, and eventually got married, and had a kid, and the kid is now the same age as my grandson - seventeen. She became involved in the local community, at the PTA, 4H, local church etc. in Wisconsin.

So, the women here in Warren County got together, and they got a copy of that ad in the magazine and had it somehow imprinted on fabric, and made a quilt with that ad imprinted in the center of it. *

And they gave it to her as a wedding present.

I suspect my wife was behind it.

PINKY

In the early 1930's, Lew "Pinky" Beers was in law school and drove a a cute, little 1924 Doctor's Coupe Model T. After graduation, he set up a practice in Phillipsburg. He wasn't an especially busy attorney, so that since he lived next door to the Shimer School, and if a teacher didn't show up he would be available at the last moment to act as a substitute. He could teach any subject because he was certificated to teach.

He wasn't a typical attorney who liked to have his picture on a billboard. Instead, he was one of the good ole redneck boys who liked to hang out at Biblehiemer's Gas Station on South Main Street and shoot the breeze with the rest of the rednecks. He kept the coupe in his buddy's barn. (This was "Dutch" Wilson Hamlen's barn on 519 just south of the Morries Acre railroad culvert). The condition was that whenever they were putting hay in the hay mow, they had to push that car out, so they didn't damage it

with the hay bales when they threw them around and put hay up in the breast mow. The breast mow was a mow over the top of the threshing floor, and the reason they call it a breast mow is because it hung out over the top.

At some point, Dr. Clarence Serfass acquired this car. He and his sons had it all fixed up - painted nicely, re-upholstered, put hydraulic brakes on it and a modern ignition system with a distributor from a Volkswagen bug, and the Serfass family was active in the Lehigh Valley Antique Car Club for many years.

Fast forward to 2017: Doc and his wife moved to a retirement facility, and they had to put the car up for sale. It just so happened that I met a guy named Paul in Jacktown who was interested in buying a Model T.

He had been looking on eBay, going to car shows, looking at the Hershey Flea Market and I told him that good friends of mine had the car he was looking for. Finally, it all came together, and he purchased the pictured Model T Ford and we took it to Paul's home.

The car's got a good home, and Serfass didn't want to see the car made into a hotrod or see it junked.

Everybody is happy.

OWED TO LIZ

It was always a pleasant encounter
To find Liz behind the NAPA counter.
She might have looked a little rough
But she really knew her stuff
Autozone kids say: "Your part does not exist."
But Liz had it on her mental list
Or took the time to really look
Through an old worn-out book.
In the Parts Man's Hall of Fame
Liz's star now burns with eternal flame
And we have lost a helpful friend
Who worked happily up to the end.

Liz Hamerstone

Born: July 20, 1957
Died: July 20, 2017

EULOGY FOR NOBERT MCGUIRE

Growing up in Pohatcong Township, I was the product of a one-room school, and a two-room school, and then I was promoted to a three-room school for eighth grade. It was a big school – it had three rooms. Our teacher was an old maid schoolteacher; or so we thought she was, only she actually got married.

One day, she sent Norbert and me downstairs to paint a map of the world; and using the paint they had in school which was like colored white-wash, we managed to paint our map…and spilled paint on the cast iron steps of the school which we wiped up a best we could. But being kids, we left evidence for the janitor to clean up.

We were brothers-in-arms. We were accomplices. We had something in common, and we were soulmates.

But, as I said, I met my match.

The next day we tried to point out to the teacher that it appeared that the coastline of Africa and the coastline of South America fit together, and she insisted that is absolutely impossible: land could not move, and it didn't say anything about that in the Bible. (Pangea had not been invented).

I continued my friendship with him throughout high school, and afterwards (after my wife and I were married) we and other couples got together at least every New Year's Eve. After he retired, he and I decided that we really should spend more time together, so every Saturday we would go someplace. We'd go to a museum, go looking for covered bridges, go take a ride on four-wheelers, go visit the steam train operation in Carpentersville. We spent a lot of time in other places, and we could always go to Barnes and Noble. We became even closer friends.

He loved words. He never had a whole lot of education; he never had a great job. He was an intelligent guy who could speak or discuss things with anybody on most any subject he was always interested in. He collected antique words and compiled a list, and I'll read a few of his expressions, OK? (See pages 173-184).

Something I never ever thought about was that it was possible for two men to love each other in a nonsexual way.

188

Dear Reader,

Welcome, I see you like to start to read from the back to the front like I normally do. It doesn't bother me a bit. Hope you like (liked) these reminisces which are about things that happened awhile back. Most are basically true and 'whimsical' creative non-fiction. I wrote a column for the Lehigh Valley Antique Car club on America for thirty years.

My bride and I went to Ireland for our fiftieth wedding anniversary, and our eldest son got into our house and put together some fifty of my stories into a booklet to give out at our anniversary party. What to do with the other stories - maybe publish another book. In this Uber-inspired society, it might be good to know that it used to be fun to drive cars, and it still is if you have an old Model T Ford and are able to find some backroads.

We all are a product of our environment, and I have always lived on a backroad on a farm and have The Great Depression philosophy of "Eat it up; wear it out; make it do, or do without'. When we got audited by the IRS, the auditor wanted to know where the checks were for our garbage pickup. I said, "Ain't got none we fed it to the dog and cats, and if they don't eat it we put it into the manure spreader and let the crows pick through it and it's gone."

I had purchased a huge, self-unloading chuckwagon (forage wagon) at a farm auction for $2,000, and recorded it as such. The IRS auditor picked this receipt up and while we were looking for the corresponding check, he said, "That certainly is a lot of money for dogfood."

So, pick through this stuff, so these tales don't get gone when I'm gone.

* * * * * * *

Most of my stories are presented as creative nonfiction loosely based on people I've known or heard about—and perhaps, should always be prefaced by the warning that the Surgeon General has ruled that it all isn't necessarily true. Like everything else today, it carries a disclaimer that any similarity to persons living or dead is purely coincidental. Also included are some fake facts.